Translated Te

This series is designed to meet the needs of students of ancient and medieval history and others who wish to broaden their study by reading source material, but whose knowledge of Latin or Greek is not sufficient to allow them to do so in the original language. Many important Late Imperial and Dark Age texts are currently unavailable in translation and it is hoped that TTH will help to fill this gap and to complement the secondary literature in English which already exists. The series relates principally to the period 300-800 AD and includes Late Imperial, Greek, Byzantine and Syriac texts as well as source books illustrating a particular period or theme. Each volume is a self-contained scholarly translation with an introductory essay on the text and its author and notes on the text indicating major problems of interpretation, including textual difficulties.

Front cover drawing: Donatist iconography, from an example found near Tebessa (source: *Buletin des Antiquaires de France* 1906, séance du 11 Avril, Heron de Villefosse

A full list of published titles in the Translated Texts for Historians series is printed at the end of this book.

Translated Texts for Historians
Volume 24

Donatist Martyr Stories
The Church in Conflict in Roman North Africa

Translated with notes and introduction by
MAUREEN A. TILLEY

Liverpool
University
Press

First published 1996
Liverpool University Press
Senate House, Abercromby Square
Liverpool, L69 3BX

Copyright © 1996 Maureen A. Tilley

British Library Cataloguing-in-Publication Data
A British Library CIP Record is available
ISBN 0-85323-931-2

Printed in the European Union by
Redwood Books, Trowbridge, England

CONTENTS

ABBREVIATIONS

AB   *Analecta Bollandiana*

ANF   *The Ante-Nicene Fathers*

CCSL   *Corpus Christianorum Series Latina*

CIL   *Corpus Inscriptionum Latinarum*

Cod. Theod.   *The Theodosian Code*. Translated with a com-
                    mentary by Clyde Pharr. Princeton: Princeton
                    University, 1952.

CSEL   *Corpus Scriptorum Ecclesiasticorum Latinorum*

Eusebius, *EH*   Eusebius, *The Ecclesiastical History*. Trans-
                    lated by J. E. L. Oulton. Loeb Classical Lib-
                    rary. Cambridge: Harvard; and London: Heine-
                    mann, 1980.

Frend, *M&P*   W. H. C. Frend. *Martyrdom and Persecution
                    in the Early Church: A Study of Conflict from
                    the Maccabees to Donatus*. New York: New
                    York University, 1967.

Frend, *TDC*   W. H. C. Frend. *The Donatist Church: A
                    Movement of Protest in Roman North Africa*.
                    Oxford: Clarendon, 1952.

Maier   *Le Dossier du Donatisme*. Edited and translated
                    by Jean-Louis Maier. T&U 135 and 135. Ber-
                    lin: Akademie-Verlag, 1987 and 1989.

Migne	*Patrologiae Cursus Completus, Series Latina.* 221 vols. Edited by Jacques Paul Migne. Paris: Garnier, 1844-94.
Monceaux	Paul Monceaux, *Histoire littéraire de l'Afrique chrétienne depuis les origines jusqu'a l'invasion arabe.* 7 vols. Paris, 1901-23; repr. Brussels: Civilisation et Culture, 1963.
Musurillo	*The Acts of the Christian Martyrs.* Introduction, texts and translations by Herbert Musurillo. Oxford: Clarendon, 1972.
Optatus	*The Work of St. Optatus Bishop of Milevis against the Donatists.* Translated by O. R. Vassall-Phillips. London and New York: Longmans Green, 1917.
PL	*Patrologiae Cursus Completus, Series Latina.* Edited by Jacques Paul Migne. 221 Vols. Paris: Garnier, 1844-94.
PW	August Friedrich von Pauly, *Paulys Realencyclopädie der classischen Alterumswissenschaft. Neue Arbeitung.* Edited by Georg Wissowa *et al.* Stuttgart: Metzler, 1893-
REA	*Revue des Études Augustiniennes*
SC	*Sources Chrétiennes*
T&U	*Texte und Untersuchungen*

PREFACE

Winning a religious war has much in common with being the victor in a military battle. Those who finally hold power enjoy carte blanche in writing the history of the campaign. The history of the Donatist-Catholic controversy among Christians in Roman North Africa is no exception. It has been viewed largely through the eyes of the Catholic victors, through the writings of Optatus of Milevis (fl. 370) and Augustine of Hippo (354-430).[1] It is not that there were no other records to read, but the victors were historically more energetic in recording, transmitting and even translating their own side of the story. Optatus and Augustine knew the value of well-turned summaries of the controversy. Even today historians have recourse to Augustine who summarized Optatus as well as the events of his own time rather than to the less succinct and explicit documents produced by the Donatist community. The result is that historians have better access to the Catholic version of the struggle and the Catholic version became *the* story of the conflict.

As early as 1934 Walter Bauer sensitized historians of early Christianity to the pitfalls of doing history only from the side of the winners.[2] Yet no one applied his wisdom to the history of the Donatist movement. Scholars continued to read a tendentious translation of Optatus and to prefer Augustine's biased summary of the last major Catholic-Donatist

---

[1] The only English translation of Optatus is *The Work of St. Optatus, Bishop of Milevis against the Donatists*, translated by O. R. Vassall-Phillips (London: Longmans, Green, and Co., 1917). A few of the Augustinian anti-Donatist treatises are found in *St. Augustin [sic]: The Writings against the Manichæans and against the Donatists*, translated by J. R. King and annotated by Chester D. Hartraft, vol. 4 of *A Select Library of the Nicene and Post-Nicene Fathers*, First Series, edited by Philip Schaff (Buffalo: Chrsitian Literature Publishing Co., 1887; repr. Peabody, MA: Hendrickson,, 1994).

[2] *Rechtgläubigkeit und Ketzerei im ältesten Christentum* (Tubingen: Mohr Siebeck, 1934), in translation as *Orthodoxy and Heresy in Earliest Christianity*, edited by Robert A. Kraft and Gerhard Krodel (Philadelphia: Fortress, 1971).

conference to the untranslated stenographic record of the proceedings.[3]
It is no wonder, then, that scholars portrayed the Donatists as an intransi-
gent, monolithic, and millennialist sect of Christianity which never
adjusted to the end of the Roman persecutions, for that is the portrait their
opponents in the fourth and fifth centuries painted of them.

Recently, however, scholars have focussed on long-neglected texts not
filtered through the sieve of Catholic polemic. Serge Lancel and Jean-
Louis Maier have provided editions of some of the germane texts for a
Francophone audience.[4] Anglophones have been less fortunate. Only
William S. Babcock has provided a translation of Donatist material in
English with his edition of Tyconius' *Liber Regularum*.[5]

The current volume of translations of the stories of Donatist martyrs
seeks to fill part of the great lacuna by providing translations of *acta* and
passiones which have never appeared in English.[6] These accounts are
especially precious in view of the paucity of surviving materials from
Donatist pens. While the stories do not constitute an historical chronicle
or 'high' theology, they do provide information which allows both
historians and theologians to verify, nuance, expand, and at times correct
Optatus and Augustine.

Before readers turn to the stories themselves, it would be well to
rehearse, first, the theoretical basis for the controversy, the specific
context for the split in African Christianity and finally, the legal and
literary background of the stories. These will be found in the "Introduc-

---

[3] *Breviculus Collationis cum Donatistis* in *Gesta Conlationis Carthaginensis, anno 411.
Accedit Sancti Augustini breviculus conlationis cum Donatistis*, edited by Serge Lancel, CCL
149A (Turnhout: Brepols, 1974), pp. 259-306, versus the *Gesta* themselves. See n. 4.

[4] Serge Lancel, *Actes de la Conférence de Carthage en 411*, 4 vols., SC 194, 195, 224
and 373 (Paris: Cerf, 1972-1991), hereafter cited as *Gesta*; and Jean-Louis Maier, *Le Dossier
du Donatisme*, 2 vols., T&U 134 and 135 (Berlin: Akademie Verlag, 1987 and 1989). For
a critical review of Maier's edition and translations, see Noël Duval, "Une nouvelle édition
du 'Dossier du Donatisme' avec traduction française," *REA* 35 (1989), pp. 171-79.

[5] *Tyconius: The Book of Rules*, Texts and Translations 31, Early Christian Literature Series
7 (Atlanta: Scholars, 1989).

[6] The story of St. Crispina was used by both Donatists and Catholics. It has been translated
by Herbert Musurillo in *The Acts of the Christian Martyrs* (Oxford: Clarendon, 1972), pp.
302-309. Because it is not characteristically Donatist and did not play a polemical role in
Donatist-Catholic controversies, it is not included here.

tion" and the "Legal and Literary Notes".

In Latin, the word 'translator' is the same as the word for 'traitor'. Lest these words be equated in this case, the discussion of two issues is in order: the word *traditor* itself and the issue of inclusive language.

The Latin word *traditor/traditores* represents those who have deserted to the side of the enemy, handing over (*tradere*) themselves and, often, state secrets to the opposition. In the context of the Donatist controversy, it bears even more weight. Assuredly, it means those Christians who left the true (in Donatist eyes) church and became members of the church affiliated with the Empire. But it meant even more. The root of the word, *tradere*, meant to hand over physical objects and that is what the original North African *traditores* did. When Roman soldiers came calling during the persecutions, ecclesiastical officials handed over the sacred books, vessels, and other church goods, rather than risk legal penalties. The *traditores* sought some accommodation with the State and relativized the importance of physical objects.

Traditionalist North Africans who would later form the Donatist movement scorned those who opted for exterior conformity to the edicts of the State. But this was not simply because they were rigorists on questions of Church and State. It was also because of their long-perduring physicalist approach to religion. The books were not merely paper and ink, wood and vellum or parchment. They were the very Word of God. Handing over the Bible and handing over the martyrs were faces of the same coin, the coin of treason to the Church.

The term *traditores* was applied not only to the persons who literally engaged in these acts, but also to their ecclesial descendants, generation after generation, i.e., the persons they ordained.[7] Hence, they were not only *traditores*, but members of the church of the *traditores*, the Catholic Church.

The stories of the martyrs in this volume are translated from the Latin

---

[7] Thus we find Petilian, the Donatist bishop of Constantine (*ca.* 395-412), aggressively questioning Augustine at the Conference of Carthage in 411 regarding his ecclesiatical parentage, i.e., who ordained him. See *Gesta* 3.227-244 (SC 224.1168-83). Considering the Catholic view on original sin which antedated even the Pelagian controversy, this must have stung. On the Catholic view, see Peter Brown, *Augustine. A Biography* (Berkeley and Los Angeles: University of California, 1967), p. 388.

sources indicated in each of the introductory sections. They are translated inclusively not simply because this is the contemporary style but for two reasons. First, the Donatists themselves valued martyrs by either sex over male hierarchical leadership. Second, Donatist exegesis is different from contemporary practice in its use of feminine metaphors and models. In the ambient Christian literature, male figures in Scripture are models for the behavior of both men and for women, and female figures model only institutions. Thus individuals, both men and women, find their models for Christian virtue only in masculine patterns. In Donatist literature, by contrast, female figures may be models for individual men's behavior. Between these two historical facts and the expectations of contemporary readers, an inclusive translation seems appropriate.

References to documents other than the Donatist martyr stories translated in this volume are to easily accessible translations. Only when no translations exist or when modern translations obscure the point made in Latin are Latin versions referenced.

In the course of writing this book, I have incurred several debts of gratitude which I am happy to acknowledge. The first is to Raymond Van Dam who encouraged the book at its start. The second is to the Florida State University. A Summer Research Grant provided the funds and the time for the acquisition, transcription and collation of microfilms of the manuscripts of *The Acts of the Abitinian Martyrs*. A sabbatical permitted the final editing and preparation of copy for the book. I owe a very large debt to Gillian Clark and Robert Markus for their diligent editing, their suggestions for the improvement of the introductory materials and footnotes, and for their encouragement through the entire process of writing and editing this volume. Finally, I would like to thank my husband, Terrence Tilley, for the preparation of the camera-ready copy of the manuscript and for all his encouragement and help along the way.

INTRODUCTION

In the city of Carthage[1] in the year 304, there was a riot outside the entrance to the prison. Christians coming in from the countryside to visit their friends and relatives in prison were pushed, shoved, whipped, and prevented from bringing consolation to the confessors confined in dark cells and tortured to the shedding of blood. The food and drink they brought for those in the dungeons were knocked from their hands and scattered where the dogs could lap them up. Parents, both fathers and mothers, were beaten into the gutters.[2]

The remarkable thing about the incident was not the riot itself; Carthage must have had its share of ruffians and violence. The noteworthy fact was that these Christian rustics were beaten not by the local Roman authorities, but by troops employed by Mensurius, the Christian bishop of the city, and by Caecilian, his deacon, who, for reasons which remain obscure, did not want these people visiting their friends and neighbors in jail. The occasion represents the first time that North African Christians conspired with the state to harass other Christians. The story of the confessors inside the prison and their reaction to the riot is preserved in *The Acts of the Abitinian Martyrs*, the story which encapsulated the outrage of the confessors and their supporters against their Christian oppressors.

This incident is key to understanding the Donatist schism. To situate the incident and, indeed, the schism itself, we need to consider the issues the incident raises.

This division of Christians against other Christians began long before the traditional date of 311 when two bishops claimed the see of Carthage. It continued for some time after the Catholics declared victory in 411. It was this split between Christian churches which found its rallying cries

---

[1] This and all other places mentioned in these stories whose locations are certain are marked on the map on p. 89.

[2] See *The Acts of the Abitinian Martyrs* §20.

in the stories of this volume.

Donatism was a religious movement which peaked in fourth-century North Africa in response to a crisis of ecclesiology. The specific point at issue was the relationship of the Christian community to the larger society. All the disputes between Catholics and Donatists were rooted in their different approaches to the matter.

Earliest Christianity had viewed the State, specifically the Roman Empire, in two ways, both of which had biblical warrants, and both of which served to strengthen the cohesion of the Christian community. Beginning with the writings of Paul and Luke and continuing with the Apologists, Christians saw the State was a necessary condition of life in the world, a manifestation of the general authority of God over creation. At best, it was a gift of God for the ordered conduct of human affairs (e.g., Rom 13.1-7). In this view, Church and State were both established by God and mutually reinforced Christian morality.

But, if fact, the general society did not see the Christian way of life as identical with the best interests of the State and, in response, Christians were perceived and perceived themselves as being at odds with the State. A second view of the relationship between Church and State developed. The State as an entity and in the person of its leader was the servant of Satan or the Antichrist in the Bible (Rev *passim*) and in the writings of Christian polemicists of the second and third centuries.

However, when Christianity became a state-supported institution, Christians were forced to rethink the relationship of the Church and the larger world. Eusebius' response, embodied especially in his *Life of Constantine*, was to take the Pauline-Lukan and apologetic tack and see the State as an instrument of the establishment of divine order. Augustine in *The City of God* saw it as a condition of temporal existence, neither sainted nor diabolical, destined to pass away at the end of the world. With the State supporting Christianity, it would seem difficult to imagine that any Christian congregation could revive the motif of the State as Antichrist. But that indeed was what Donatism did when, as we shall see, the State assisted Catholic Christians in persecuting Donatist Christians, a revolution in Christian history.

The Abitinian incident at Carthage reveals one of the prime facts about most North African Christians, at least up to the beginning of the fourth century. These Christians were proud of the members of their Church who had suffered for their faith and they treasured their personal associations with these champions. From the days of the Scillitan martyrs (*ca.* 188) and Perpetua and Felicity (203) to the era of Cyprian (mid-third century), fidelity under trying circumstances provided a point of self-definition for North African Christians.[3] The experience of group solidarity in persecution helped to define them against their non-Christian neighbors.

Defiance of persecution also defined faithful Christians against their lax co-religionists who had cooperated with the civil authorities in times of repression. Persecutions under Decius (249-251) and Valerian (253-260) cemented the connection between opposition to the state and truly faithful adherence to Christianity. The result was an identification of martyrdom with Christianity and a diminished tolerance for lapsed Christians seeking to return to the Church.[4] Later, Donatists of the fourth and fifth centuries would look back to this period for models of behavior and guidance. The bishop-martyr Cyprian would be their hero and they would circulate *The Donatist Passion of Saint Cyprian* as an inspiration for their own times.

But at the end of the third and beginning of the fourth centuries, imperial protection or persecution of Christians was not a question in and for itself. Rather Emperors and Caesars used religious groups as game pieces in the contest for ultimate power.[5] There was peace when the emperors were otherwise distracted, but repression returned when opportune for one imperial party or another. During the persecutions under Diocletian (303-305), there were new martyrs whose stories left a legacy of intransigence to the Donatist movement. These include *The Acts of Saint Felix Bishop and Martyr*, *The Passion of Saints Maxima, Donatilla and Secunda*, and the most influential of all Donatist stories, *The Acts of the Abitinian Martyrs*.

After 312 when Christianity was no longer a proscribed religion, Constantine considered it his religious duty as emperor to support Christian worship along with other recognized cults. For example, he provided

---

[3] These early martyr stories are collected in Musurillo.

[4] On the contemporary hesitancy of bishop Cyprian to reconcile lax Christians on any but the most stringent terms, see *St. Cyprian. The Lapsed. The Unity of the Catholic Church*, translation and commentary by Maurice Bèvenot, Ancient Christian Writers 25 (Westminster, Maryland: Newman; and London: Longmans, Green, 1957).

[5] See Timothy D. Barnes, *Constantine and Eusebius* (Cambridge: Harvard, 1981).

subsidies for Christian worship and freed upper-class Christian priests from their time-consuming and financially draining duties of serving in municipal government.[6] Keeping peace among Christianity's various factions was also Constantine's duty, one recognized by Christians themselves who appealed to him to arbitrate their disputes. The Donatist controversy was the first of these conflicts.

The controversy began in the divisions between Christians over the seriousness of a Christian succumbing to pressure in persecution and handing over the Scriptures to be burnt or sacrificing as prescribed by law. The division was already obvious in the events of the early fourth century, like the fracas at Carthage in the reaction to Mensurius' conduct, and in 305[7] when some North African Christians tried to keep bishops who had been *traditores* (those who had handed over the Scriptures to be burnt) from being electors of bishops in other dioceses. Partisans of the hard line were especially numerous in Numidia. However, at that time in the direct aftermath of the persecution, even in Numidia, the value of Church unity won out over ecclesiastical purity and at least one bishop who may have handed over the Scriptures and another who had been a murderer were allowed to participate in the election of the bishop of a vacant see.[8]

Six years later, in 311, values were being reversed: those who handed over the Scriptures were no longer welcome in many quarters. While popular schism, the split into tolerant and rigorist parties, had begun years earlier, by 311 the hardening of attitudes eventuated in institutional schism. In that year Mensurius the bishop of Carthage died. The contemporary procedure for succession in North Africa was that twelve bishops of the

---

[6] Eusebius, *EH* 10.6.1-2 (2.460-462) and 10.7.1-2 (2.462-464).

[7] On the establishment of the date of 305, see Maier, p. 114, n. 16; and Serge Lancel, "Les débuts du Donatisme: la date du 'Protocole de Cirta' et de l'élection épiscopale de Silvanus," *REA* 25 (1979), pp. 217-29.

[8] See the proceedings of the Council of Cirta, in *the Acts of the Council of Cirta* in *Optatus* (*Optatus*, Appendix XI, Vassall-Phillips, 416-420). For a related incident regarding traditores in 320, cf. *The Proceedings before Zenophilus* (*Optatus*, Appendix II, Vassall-Phillips pp. 346-381). Both are found in Maier, pp. 115-118 and 211-239, respectively.

region would gather to elect a successor.[9] By custom the Primate of Numidia presided. But before any Numidian bishops could make the trek to Carthage, the Carthaginians pushed ahead with the election. The rigorists who predominated in Numidia were not given a chance to participate in choosing a new bishop of Carthage. Members of the tolerant party at Carthage tried to head off trouble by quickly electing one of their own.

But even at Carthage Christians were already polarized over Mensurius for his treatment of imprisoned Christians and for the suspicion that he had handed over Scriptures to be burned. His deacon and eventual successor, Caecilian, was similarly suspect for his cooperation in Mensurius' interdiction of supplies for prisoners at Carthage. Traditionalists opposed his eventual election on the grounds that he was guilty of non-support, i.e., persecution, of the martyrs, and that one of his consecrators, Felix of Apthugni, had been one of the *traditores*. Carthaginian traditionalists together with the Numidians elected their own bishop of Carthage, Majorinus, who was eventually succeeded by Donatus, giving the movement its name, Donatism.

More was at stake than simply who occupied the episcopal throne. There were external considerations, such as recognition by the churches of other cities and recognition by the imperial court. So Donatists appealed to Constantine for adjudication of this contested election and the rights to imperial subsidies. In response he appointed a commission of bishops which sat at Rome in 313 and an appeals commission which met at Arles in 314. Both vindicated Caecilian's election.

When Donatists persisted in their rejection of the decision of the appeals commission, Constantine countered with the repression of those who refused to recognize the imperially-backed bishop of Carthage. From periods of especially severe repression, specifically from 317 to 321 and from 346 to 348, come the stories of the martyrs of Donatism. During the first period, the state confiscated Donatist churches and sent some of

---

[9] Cyprian *Ep.* 67.4 in *ANF*, Vol. 5: *Fathers of the Third Century: Hippolytus, Cyprian, Caius, Novatian, Appendix*, translated by A. Cleveland Coxe (Grand Rapids: Eerdmans, repr. 1981), pp. 370-371; confirmed by the Council of Carthage §39 in 397 (Frend, *TDC*, p. 12).

their bishops into exile. The persecution was intense. At one point a whole congregation was slaughtered inside a Carthaginian basilica. However, the persecution was concentrated in coastal areas where Donatists were probably not an overwhelming majority. On the whole, the military actions against the Donatists were unsuccessful. They merely succeeded in creating heroic Donatist martyrs instead of subservient new Catholics. From this first period of persecution comes *A Sermon on the Passion of Saints Donatus and Advocatus*.

In 321, faced with the failure of the campaign and more pressing military concerns, Constantine suspended the laws against the Donatists.

During the next quarter century, 321-346, Donatists and Catholics achieved a *modus vivendi*. Some areas were primarily Catholic, others Donatist. In some places both parties lived and prayed side by side in the same towns with one church for each group. Double lines of bishops succeeded one another with only occasional quarrels. During this period Donatists increased in number, especially in Numidia. They sent bishops to Rome to head an already existing Donatist congregation and they established themselves in Spain.[10] Donatism grew without significant state interference until 346.

In that year Donatus, leader of the Donatist congregations in the capital city, appealed to the emperor to follow the protocol established after the Council of Arles in 314. It had provided that when the bishop of a city died, the next senior bishop, Donatist or Catholic, should be recognized as Primate. He appealed to the emperor for recognition as senior bishop of Carthage over Gratus, his Catholic counterpart, who had occupied his see a shorter time than he had.

In response, the reigning emperor, Constans, sought advice from Hosius, bishop of Cordoba. Hosius had been his father Constantine's theological advisor. On the counsel of Hosius, Constans sent imperial notaries Paul and Macarius, with their troops, to investigate and to pacify the countryside. They harassed Donatists both in the coastal areas around Carthage and in the foothills of Numidia where Donatists probably formed a substantial majority. As a result of their investigation, on August 15, 347, the Proconsul at Carthage issued an imperial decree confirming the

---

[10] Frend, *TDC*, pp. 159-61.

Catholic bishop Gratus as sole head of the Church at Carthage and requiring all Christians to recognize him rather than Donatus as their bishop. The wording of the decree itself does not survive but later martyr stories refer to it.

The result of the Macarian campaign (346-348) was the renewal of sectarian strife, the creation of a new crop of martyrs, and the composition of new martyr stories. From this period come the last two stories in this volume, *The Passion of Maximian and Isaac* and *The Martyrdom of Marculus*.

In 348 or 349 bishop Gratus celebrated the pacification of North Africa with a grand gesture of conciliation. He affirmed the participation of both Donatists and Catholics in the council he called and admitted there had been errors on both sides. But this was not the end of the Donatist controversy. Parties named Donatist and Catholic squared off against each other in the latter half of the fourth century and, despite reports of their demise after the imperial repression of 411-20, they continued to exist. But the issue over which they fought was submerged under more pressing concerns as the Vandals marched across North Africa from Spain in the 420s. Although the name 'Donatist' perdures as a term of opprobrium until the era of Gregory the Great (*ca.* 540-604), the issues of the schism do not seem to have been vital for North Africans after 450.[11] In the face of the Vandal occupation, the urgent needs of the day pushed older issues into oblivion and the movement seems to have produced no more martyr literature.

The seven stories of this volume are the only surviving Donatist hagiographies. However, as the product of Donatist pens, they allow scholars to penetrate the history of a community largely obscured by the propaganda of the victors. To assist historians in analyzing these materials, the next chapter provides legal and literary background notes.

---

[11] For an analysis of literature regarding Donatism after the Vandal invasion, see Robert A. Markus, "The Problem of 'Donatism' in the sixth century," in his collected essays, *Sacred and Secular: Studies on Augustine and Latin Christianity* (Aldershot, Hampshire: Variorum, 1994); and his essays collected in *From Augustine to Gregory the Great: History and Christianity in Late Antiquity* (London: Variorum, 1983).

LITERARY AND LEGAL NOTES

The stories of Donatist martyrs reflect the legal situation in which the government prosecuted those who adhered to outlawed organizations or who failed to perform religious actions required by the State, at least in North Africa. Their narratives reflect the laws, customs, and literature of another place and another time. This chapter details the contextual issues for a responsible reading of the stories of the Donatist martyrs, narratives composed in a culture different from our own. There are three issues especially important for the historian. The first is the genre of the stories. The second is the degree to which the stories actually reflect the events of the time. The two issues are intimately connected, but for the sake of elucidation, we explore them one at a time. The final topic is torture. Scenes of torture appear in nearly every story of martyrdom. Both the necessity and utility of torture were taken for granted by many peoples of antiquity. Hagiographers seem to revel in recounting the methods of torture and their gory results. Since torture is one of the elements of martyr stories most repugnant to contemporary readers, it deserves a few words to help assess its place in the stories which follow.

GENRE

The first question is the literary form of the stories. The traditional answer is that they are *acta* or *passiones*, depending on the origin of the accounts and the focal points of the narratives.

In the classic division, *acta* focus on the interrogation of the martyrs in judicial or quasi-judicial proceedings. Roman courts of the period of anti-Christian persecution employed stenographers who took notes, transcribed them, and deposited the transcripts in the offices of local government so that the record of the trial might be preserved for administrative purposes. The general public was apparently allowed access to the records. Thus even when the interrogation of confessors took place *in camera*, their supporters did have access to the proceedings. In this respect they were no different from the supporters of other political prisoners.[1]

Martyrs' stories based on these proceedings tend to concentrate on the interrogation of the martyr. They may contain only the shortest of introductions and summary notices of the executions of the martyrs after they are sentenced to death. In this collection *The Donatist Passion of Cyprian* and *The Acts of Saint Felix Bishop and Martyr* exemplify the genre.

The monotony of the genre *acta* is conditioned, in part, by the legal proceedings themselves. One had to establish the identity of the accused, the nature of the charges, and the evidence for conviction (or acquittal). Dialogue between the presiding judicial officer and the defendant may seem terse and formulaic, for indeed it was. Court stenographers may have made it even more so in the transcription process.

Besides the obvious constraints of the judicial procedure, Christians also contributed to the formulation of the genre. If the *acta* are based on the minutes of the trials, they are not necessarily identical with those minutes. Recourse to a written resource is not the same thing as copying the resource verbatim. Even in antiquity, there is evidence that the *acta* were edited for Christian purposes.[2] Yet the reader should not discount the monotony of the *acta* as attributable only to either court procedure or hagiographic love of formulae, or even simply to both. In real life Christians were also specifically trained to give 'appropriate' responses. Examples of these formulae are Cyprian's "Praise God" or Maxima's "Thanks be to God."[3] Their repetition makes the story even more formulaic.

Passiones, by contrast, concentrate on the passions or sufferings and

---

[1] Trials *in camera* would have been contrary to law but not to custom. See *Cod. Theod.* 1.16.6 (Pharr, p. 28). On the presence of secretaries or stenographers who took minutes of the trials whether Christian or not, see Giuliana Lanata, *Gli atti dei martiri come documenti processuali* (Milan: Giuffrè, 1973), pp. 12-15. On the use of the *acta* in intra-Christian disputes, see Giuliana Lantana, *Processi contra Christiani negli atti dei martiri*, 2nd ed. (Turin: G. Giappichelli, 1989), pp. 6-10; and Augustine, *Breviculus collationis* 3.17.52 (CSEL 53.81).

[2] See Augustine, *Contra Cresconius*, 3.70.80 (CSEL 52.485), who acknowledges both Christian access to proconsular archives and the edited use of the materials; and Lanata, *Processi*, pp. 11-13.

[3] *The Donatist Passion of Cyprian* and *The Passion of Saints Maxima, Donatilla and Secunda* (hereafter *The Passion of Maxima*) §6.

deaths of the martyrs. These will be distinguished not by their record of
interrogations, but by their descriptions of the tortures endured by the
martyrs. Again the descriptions of the tortures themselves may seem all
too similar from one story to another. They are so unlike modern stories
of torture which are excruciatingly individual in their accounting of the
abuse which victims suffer.[4] In this volume *The Martyrdom of Marculus*
is representative of the genre *passio*.

Some stories contain both the record of judicial interrogations and
accounts of the tortures and deaths of the martyrs. Here the example is
the *Passion of Maximian and Isaac*.

These stories point out the disadvantages of too strict a dichotomy
between *acta* and *passiones*: there are simply too many pieces which do
not neatly fit either category. The later in time a piece was written, the
more often it may not fall into the patterns expected for either genre. As
martyrdom itself became more rare, the stories of martyrs came to be used
for purposes other than recording the progress of an event or exhorting
others to martyrdom. Here *A Sermon Given on the Passion of Saints
Donatus and Advocatus* is an especially good example because it is
primarily that, a sermon. Folded into this exhortation of catechumens to
heroic virtue is a politicized reading of the slaughter of Donatist partisans
in their cathedral at Carthage. The author does not rejoice in martyrdom
for its own sake, but as an attractive lure to capture the zeal of catechumens for the larger Donatist movement.

In addition to *acta*, *passiones* and sermons, martyr stories may take the
forms of panegyrics, diaries, letters, and combinations of all of the
above.[5]

Thus the historian cannot simply divide these stories into *acta* and
passiones. Moreover, if form follows function, the interpretation of these
texts must address the role the stories played in their communities. Surely
they were written to record the stories of the sufferings and deaths of the
martyrs. *The Acts of the Abitinian Martyrs* §1 makes this explicit. But to
what end? They were not written merely to preserve the memory of those

---

[4] See Maureen A. Tilley, "The Ascetic Body and the (Un)making of the World of the
Martyr, *Journal of the American Academy of Religion* 59/3 (1991), pp. 467-479.

[5] For a discussion of the various forms, see Lanata, *Gli atti*, pp. 2-14.

who died. Were that the case, they would all be careful of the dating and circumstances of death.

Rather, the accounts of the martyrdoms were written primarily to inspire Christians who needed to be able to withstand the daily threat of exposure as people different from their neighbors (because they were), as citizens subject to harassment by the larger community and punishment by the State. Of course, inspiration might take many forms. It might be direct and instructional. The stories might say: "This is how you reply to your captors; this is how you endure torture; this is how you pray when you think you can't stand the pain." It might be indirect and motivational: "See how much the martyrs suffered. How can you complain about mere civil harassment? Take them as your models in your daily resistance to the pressure to conform to your larger culture." *The Sermon on the Passion of Saints Donatus and Advocatus* is a prime example of this persuasion to resistance.

LEGISLATION AGAINST CHRISTIANS

If form follows function and Donatist hagiography is not merely some von Rankean retelling of the facts, what relation do these stories bear to the events of their times? Answering this question is a difficult task because the historian has only a very limited amount of data on the Donatist controversy beyond that generated by the Donatists themselves. In most cases, this material comes from their Catholic opponents, Optatus of Milevis and Augustine of Hippo, who themselves were at the distance of a generation or more from the earlier phases of the Donatist movement. But these sources can be interpreted and supplemented by materials from law codes, contemporary historians, and the stories of martyrs venerated on both sides, like Maxima and the Abitinians.

The notes that follow are designed to assist the historian in the evaluation of the incidents narrated in the stories of the Donatist martyrs. The first set deals with the nexus of Church and State, the second with the enforcement of the laws relating to persecution, and the third with the use of torture in interrogation.

PRESUPPOSITIONS REGARDING CHURCH AND STATE

The most important factor in evaluating religious persecution in the Roman empire, whether of Donatists or others, is the degree to which Church and State were entwined. Roman religion presumed that the people of a state and the local worshipping community were for all intents and purposes indistinguishable. Peace with heaven was the *sine qua non* of security on earth. Individuals within the community might have multiple allegiances but all would coalesce when the interests of the state were at stake. In situations of crisis, failure to participate in the religious traditions of the state would be tantamount to treason. This attitude allowed both the general persecution of Christians before Constantine and the specific attacks on Donatists after the recognition of Christianity as a legal religion.

During the persecutions under Valerian in the middle of the third century, reported in *The Donatist Passion of Cyprian*, there was a general feeling among practitioners of traditional Roman religions that the world was in a dismal state. The complaint of corruption within the state was a perennial one, but the situation seemed worse than usual as various migrating peoples were about to breach the Rhine, the Danube and the Euphrates all simultaneously. Traditional standards had to be upheld.

Similarly, the closing years of the reign of Diocletian, represented by *The Acts of Saint Felix Bishop and Martyr*, *The Passion of Saints Maxima, Donatilla and Secunda*, and *The Acts of the Abitinian Martyrs*, saw attempts at general moral reform. The emperor tightened discipline in the army, reformed the system of taxation, renewed his support for state religion, all in a bid to renew the unity and vitality of the empire. The persecution of non-conformist Christians was a natural corollary. They suffered both as scapegoats and as the objects of power politics in disputes between Diocletian and his co-emperor and caesars.

Constantine's accession in 311 did not alter the ground rules. The cohesion between Church and State did not change during the period represented by *A Sermon on the Passion of Saints Donatus and Advocatus*. Christianity became an official religion of the empire and the union of state and religion intensified. If the emperor were to keep the peace with the gods, the addition of yet another divinity did not change his responsibilities; it magnified them. He became bishop for those who had no

bishop.[6] And when Christians quarreled about doctrine or worship, it was
incumbent on him to make peace among them so that serene and proper
worship might be offered their God.

Christians too expected Constantine to be an arbitrator in religious
disputes. He acknowledged this responsibility by mediating the Catholic-
Donatist conflict through the council he appointed at Rome under Pope
Miltiades in 313 (barely six months after his acknowledgment of Christianity) and the appellant council at Arles in 314. He articulated his own
understanding of this in a letter to Aelafius, a Christian official of North
Africa, written *ca.* 314:

> Since I am informed that you too are a worshipper of the Highest
> God, I will confess to your gravity that I consider it absolutely
> contrary to the divine law that we should overlook such quarrels and
> contentions whereby the Highest Divinity may perhaps be moved to
> wrath not only against the human race, but also against me, to whose
> care He had by his celestial will committed the government of all
> earthly things, and that He may be so far moved as to take some
> untoward step. For I shall really fully be able to feel secure and
> always to hope for prosperity and happiness from the ready kindness
> of the most mighty God, only when I see all venerating the most Holy
> God in the proper cult of the catholic religion with harmonious
> brotherhood of worship.[7]

Thus it was Constantine's religious and imperial duty—as if the two could
be separated—to induce the religious conformity of the Donatists.

Constantine's son Constans carried on the tradition of State involvement
with religion. In the final period represented in this collection, the era of
The Passion of Maximian and Isaac and *The Martyrdom of Marculus*, the

---

[6] Eusebius, *Life of Constantine* 4.24 in *A Select Library of the Christian Church: Nicene
and Post-Nicene Fathers*, second series, edited by Philip Schaff and Henry Wace, Vol. 1:
*Eusebius: Church History, Life of Constantine the Great, and Oration in Praise of Con-
stantine*, translated by Arthur Cushman McGiffert (N. p. [Buffalo]: Christian Literature
Company, 1890; repr. Peabody, MA: Hendrickson, 1994), p. 546.

[7] Constantine to Aelafius in Appendix 3 of *Optatus*, p. 384; translated by Frend in *M&P*,
399-400.

concerns of the emperor for public order stemmed directly from his intervention in a religious dispute at the request of the Donatists in *ca.* 346. Their request for his mediation was based on the council convened by Constantine under Miltiades in 313. Miltiades had attempted to bring peace to North Africa and some resolution to the situations which resulted when there were two rivals, one Catholic and one Donatist, for a single see. The agreement reached at the Council had provided that the senior bishop would be recognized as the head of the Church in that city. It would not matter if the bishop belonged to the party which had supported Mensurius the Catholic or Majorinus the Donatist. The senior claimant would rule.[8] When the Catholic bishop of Carthage died thirty-three years later, Donatus the Great was then the senior claimant, and Gratus, the newly elected Catholic bishop, the junior. Donatus appealed to the emperor for acknowledgment as occupant of the see. Frend writes:

> The Emperor [Constans] did not reject Donatus' approach out of hand. As his father had done before him, he decided to send a commission to Africa to investigate and report. Two imperial notables, Paul and Macarius, were chosen for the duty and probably reached Africa in the spring of 347.[9]

Because of the perception of their bias toward the Catholics, members of the commission met an increasingly hostile response in North Africa. About the middle of 347 Constans grew impatient and decided to promulgate an edict of unity calling for the fusion of the Catholics and the Donatists with the distribution of the churches and other resources of the Donatists to the Catholics. As Monceaux notes, this was nothing new, but a reapplication of Constantine's edict against Donatists (from 317) which had never been formally abrogated.[10]

In all of the situations reflected in these stories of martyrs, imperial law was a response not only to issues of public order but also to the order of Heaven which demanded an imperial response.

---

[8] Optatus 3.3 (Vassall-Phillips, p. 136).

[9] Frend, *TDC*, p. 177.

[10] Monceaux 4.35 commenting on *Cod. Theod.* 16.6.2 (Pharr, pp. 463-64).

LEGAL MEASURES IN CONTEXT

What exactly were the legal measures promulgated against Christians? What did they proscribe and command? How were the laws enforced in North Africa? In general, one can say that, aside from mob action and the reactions of provincial and local officials to civic disturbances, the will of the emperors provided the legislative basis for the persecution of Christians in both the immediate pre-Constantinian period and the era of the Donatists in the fourth century. It was up to the imperial staff in the provinces to publicize the legislation in their areas. As we shall see, one cannot always assume that because an emperor issued an edict, the legislation was necessarily enforced or even promulgated in a particular locality. But if the legislation had been publicized in a province or a town, it was the responsibility of the local authorities to enforce the laws. The enforcement might be even-handed or not. Rank and social connections brought their privileges even when all were citizens after 212.

As in the previous section, we shall review what is known about the legislation and its enforcement in North Africa during each of the periods represented by the martyr stories in this volume.

The texts of the laws from the Valerianic persecutions in the 250s do not survive. However, from the letters of Cyprian and the stories of contemporary martyrs, one can construct the following sequence. In response to general panic at the invasion of the empire by the Goths and to the particular incident where Christians supposedly refused to come to the defense of the empire in Pontus, Valerian retaliated against Christians throughout the empire.[11] In August 257 he issued his first edict requiring all of the clergy to offer sacrifice. Cyprian refused to sacrifice and was exiled.[12] Others were sent to the mines.[13] Perhaps Cyprian's social class and connections with the Carthaginian town counsellors delayed the enforcement of any severe penalties and eventually ensured his trial before the proconsul.

In the summer of 258 the emperor redoubled his efforts. According to

---

[11] Frend, *M&P*, p. 317.

[12] Cyprian, *Ep.* 35.1 (ANF 5.314) and *The Donatist Passion of Cyprian.*

[13] Cyprian, *Ep.* 76 (ANF 5.402-404).

Cyprian:

> Valerian has sent a rescript to the Senate, to the effect that bishops
> and presbyters and deacons should immediately be punished [if they
> do not sacrifice]; but that senators, and men of importance, and
> Roman knights, should lose their dignity and moreover be deprived
> of their property; and if, when their means were taken away, they
> should persist in being Christians, they should also lose their heads;
> but that matrons should be deprived of their property, and sent into
> banishment. Moreover, people of Caesar's household, whoever of
> them had either confessed before, or should now confess, should have
> their property confiscated, and should be sent in chains by assignment
> [as slaves] to Caesar's estates.[14]

From Cyprian's letters we know that both pieces of legislation were
enforced in Carthage. There were local commissions to supervise the
sacrifices as there had been under Decius. Certificates of compliance,
libelli, would have been issued there as they were in various parts of the
empire.[15]

Persecutions continued until the Emperor's attention was drawn to a
more pressing problem, his campaign against the Persians. When Valerian's death on the Persian frontier became known at Rome on August
6, 260, his son Gallienus abandoned the harassment of the Christians.[16]

Historians are better informed about the persecutions at the turn of the
fourth century. They appear to be part of a return to traditional values
which affected such aspects of general culture as monetary policy and
marriage laws.[17] Martyrdoms began when Maximian engaged in a campaign for the restoration of strict discipline in the army which at this time
included many Christians.[18] Several stories of military martyrs survive
from the period 295 to 299 when the emperor was visiting North Africa.

---

[14] *Ep.* 81.1 (ANF 5.408).
[15] Cyprian, *On the Lapsed* 7 (ANF 5.439) and *Epp.* 18 and 19 (ANF 5.297).
[16] Eusebius, *EH* 7.13 (Loeb 2.268-70). Cf. Frend, *M&P*, p. 500, n. 136, on the date.
[17] Frend, *M&P*, pp. 351-54.
[18] Eusebius, *EH* 7.13.1 (Loeb 2.168-70) and Frend, *M&P*, p. 359.

These include Maximilian and Marcellus of Theveste[19] and Typasius and Fabius in Caesarea Mauretania.[20] But as Paul Monceaux notes, these men were not executed specifically for being Christians but for their refusal to conform to military discipline.[21] They had refused either induction or recall.

The general persecutions began at the orders of Diocletian issued on February 23, 303. His edict was published a little later in the West under the jurisdiction of Maximian.[22] This first measure called for the destruction of churches and the burning of sacred books. It prohibited holding Christian assembly and forbade Christians to hold public office. According to Lactantius, there were other rights lost:

> [I]n civil life *honestiores* were to lose their important privileges of birth and status, and no Christian might act as accuser in cases of personal injury, adultery and theft. Christian slaves might no longer be freed. Only the lives of the sectaries were spared; otherwise they were to be outlawed.[23]

While we are better informed regarding enforcement in the East (thanks to Eusebius), we do know something of patterns of enforcement in Africa. This first edict was promulgated in Proconsularis in mid-April of 303.[24] It was enforced throughout the Spring in North Africa. Some bishops acceded to imperial demands for church property. Others, like bishop Felix, resisted. A fortnight after the edict's promulgation in Thibiuca, he

---

[19] Musurillo, pp. 244-59.

[20] Both are contained in "Passiones Tres Martyrum Africanorum," edited by Charles de Smedt, *AB* 9 (1890), pp. 107-34.

[21] Monceaux 3.26-28.

[22] On the dates, see Lactantius, *On the Manner in which the Persecutors Died* 12 in *The Ante-Nicene Fathers*, edited by Alexander Roberts and James Donaldson, Vol. 7: *Lactantius, Venantius, Asterius, Victorinus, Dionysius, Apostolic Teaching and Constitutions, 2 Clement, Early Liturgies*, translated by A. Cleveland Coxe (Bufffalo: Christian Literature Publishing, 1886; repr. Peabody, MA: Hendrickson, 1994), p. 305; and Monceaux 3.28.

[23] Lactantius 13 (ANF 7.306) and Eusebius *EH* 8.2.4 (Loeb 2.258).

[24] See Frend, *M&P*, p. 372.

was martyred on the 15th of June.[25]

In his second edict, sent out in the summer of 303, Diocletian called on provincial governors to arrest and imprison the clergy. The third edict called for the clergy to offer sacrifice. If they did so, they were to be released.[26] These two measures do not seem to have been enforced anywhere in North Africa. There is no indication that clergy were brought in separately from anyone else. In fact, when they do appear in narratives, it is along with other distinguished citizens, with no particular separation of clergy from laity.[27]

The fourth edict of this persecution was not issued by Diocletian, but by Galerius during Diocletian's illness. This edict called for all persons to offer sacrifice. It was issued in the East in the Spring of 304, ratified by the Senate April 22, 304, and was promulgated in the West in the summer of that same year.[28] While there is no direct evidence of the promulgation of the edict in North Africa, it was obviously the legal measure underlying the persecution, because those who were executed in 304 were asked not whether they had scriptures to surrender but whether they would offer sacrifice.[29]

In the cases of both of the first and fourth edicts, the only ones promulgated in North Africa under Diocletian, the usual initial enforcement was not in the hands of imperial appointees but of local officials whatever they were called: at Thibiuca it was the curator Magnilianus; in Abitina, it was the local magistrates accompanied by a soldier stationed in the area.[30] However, the edicts were not uniformly enforced. In one case, a breakdown in communication occasioned a delay in enforcement. Alfius Caecilianus, the duumvir of Apthugni, apparently never received direct instruc-

---

[25] See *The Proceedings before Zenophilus* in Optatus (Vassall-Phillips, pp. 352-54) where church officials assist in the inventory of property for confiscation, and the *Martyrdom of Felix Bishop and Martyr.*

[26] Eusebius, *EH* 8.2.5 and 8.6.8-10 (Loeb 2.258 and 2.268).

[27] See *The Acts of the Abitinian Martyrs* §2, *The Acts of Saint Felix* §1, and *The Passion of Maxima* §1.

[28] Frend, *M&P*, p. 366; and Monceaux 3.28.

[29] *The Passion of Maxima* §1 and *The Martyrdom of Crispina* §1 (Musurillo, p. 302); cf. Frend, *M&P*, p. 375, commenting on *Crispina.*

[30] *The Acts of Saint Felix* §1 and *The Acts of the Abitinian Martyrs* §2.

tions to enforce the first or the fourth edict. He heard of the first edict, or perhaps saw a copy, while travelling in other cities. Without further guidelines, he began enforcing it in his own town.[31]

In several other cases, martyr stories report enforcement by imperial authorities in towns and rural areas, e.g., the proconsuls Anulinus of Proconsularis in areas outside Carthage[32] and Florus of Numidia at Mascula.[33] There are several reasons why provincial rather than local officials might enforce the edicts. Some local officials were simply unable to enforce the edicts. The *curator* of Thibiuca and officials at Cirta, for example, had trouble finding anyone to give them information on the whereabouts of the persons who knew the location of the Christian scriptures which were to be burned.[34] Frend suggests that local officials and the clergy colluded to obstruct justice.[35] Of course, it is possible that a hagiographer sought to dignify the individual martyrs by having their first court room appearances as well as the eventual condemnations take place in the presence of the most important provincial official.

Perhaps the most likely reason for the regular literary appearance of the proconsul is that proconsuls did indeed try local cases referred to them. When a proconsul toured a province, local officials could show their loyalty by demonstrating in his presence that they were indeed enforcing the edicts which he had forwarded to them. *The Passion of Saints Maxima, Donatilla et Secunda* provides evidence for this hypothesis. According to the story, the young women were arraigned before Anulinus when he was at a country estate where all the people were making a great show of their loyalty to the empire by sacrificing. He left the estate the next day without finishing the interrogations of Maxima and Donatilla, so he had them brought along with his entourage to Thuburbo, his next stop. Similarly

---

[31] *The Proceedings before Zenophilus* in Optatus, Appendix 2 (Vassall-Phillips, p. 334).

[32] *The Passion of Maxima* §1 on a country estate near Thuburbo, and *The Martyrdom of Crispina* §1 (Musurillo, p. 302) at Theveste.

[33] Augustine, *Contra Cresconium* 3.27.30 in *S. Aureli Augustini Scripta contra Donatistas*, CSEL 51-53, edited by M. Petschenig (Vienna: Tempsky; and Leipzig: Freytag, 1908-10), 52.436.

[34] *The Acts of Felix Bishop and Martyr* §1; and *The Proceedings before Zenophilus* (Vassall-Phillips, pp. 353 and 355-56). Cf. Monceaux 3.34.

[35] Frend, *TDC*, pp. 230-32.

The Acts of the Abitinian Martyrs §§3-4 suggests that arraignment took place before a local magistrate but that he did not have the staff and facilities to question them under torture. Finally, the best reason is that capital crimes were by law referred to imperial officials for execution of the death sentence.[36]

By the end of 304 the worst was over in North Africa. Although persecutions continued intermittently until 311, details are available only for the East. The empire does not seem to have made more martyrs in North Africa between 304 and Constantine's accession.

Between the legalization of Christianity in 313 and the beginning of the persecution of Donatists was a four-year span. During this time Christianity was treated as a *religio licita*, a recognized and protected religion. As such it could expect support from the imperial administration. But when institutional divisions between Christian groups occurred in 311, Constantine had to choose sides. Under the influence of his theological advisor, Hosius of Corduba, Constantine favored Catholic Christians over Donatists. In North Africa he distributed money and favors (such as immunity from civic levies) only to those bishops in communion with Caecilian, the Catholic bishop of Carthage.[37] Repeated Donatist appeals produced no change in Constantine's position. His attitude hardened and he began to describe the Donatists as "certain persons of unstable mind . . . desirous of turning aside the laity of the most holy Catholic Church by some vile seduction." He authorized Caecilian to turn them over to judicial authority.[38]

The persecution of Donatists began in earnest in May 317.[39] Constantine sent funds to Africa to award to Donatist congregations which declared themselves in communion with Caecilian. He placed both civil and military authority at the beck and call of Caecilian: the *comes* Ursatius

---

[36] *Cod. Theod.* 1.16.1 (Pharr, p. 27); cf. G. E. M. de Ste Croix, "Why Were the Early Christians Persecuted?" in *Studies in Ancient Society*, edited by M. I. Finley in the *Past and Present Series*, edited by Trevor Aston (London and Boston: Routledge and Kegan Paul, 1974), pp. 210-49, specifically p. 217, on the earlier tradition of the reservation of capital crimes under the Principate.

[37] Eusebius, *EH* 10.6.1-5 (Loeb 2.454-56).

[38] Eusebius *EH* 10.6.4-5 (Loeb 2.463).

[39] On the dating, see Frend, *M&P*, p. 316.

and the *dux* Leontius were at his disposal to bring Donatists to justice as those who disturbed the order of the Catholic Church.[40] One piece of legislation surviving from this period calls for the incarceration of Donatists whose only crime was producing controversial literature. Even if they could prove that the charges that they made against Catholics were true, they were not to be released.[41] The sole issue was the disturbance of public order—and that included religious order.

The only other legal documentation from this first wave of anti-Donatist persecution is Constantine's letter of May 5, 321, to the bishops and the people of the African church. In the letter he acknowledged that his use of force had not accomplished the end for which it was begun, i.e., peace, stability and concord. He ordered an end to the use of military force against the Donatists until Heaven revealed to him some more effective option.[42] Meanwhile his troops were needed elsewhere.

African Christians worked out their own *modus vivendi*, maintaining two congregations in many towns, one Catholic and the other Donatist. When Constans intervened again in 346, he followed the same course as his father. He sent Paul and Macarius, imperial notaries, with funds to distribute to loyal congregations—which the Donatists interpreted as a bribe[43]—and military might to back up an investigation of other congregations. On August 15, 347, faced with increasing African opposition to the Macarian commission, Constans voided Constantine's suspension of the laws against the Donatists issued in 321. He imposed an edict of unity with the threat of torture and exile.[44] In November of 347 Donatist bishops sent to Macarius a committee of their own to explore options and to plead

---

[40] *A Sermon Given on the Passion of Saints Donatus and Advocatus* (hereafter *The Passion of Donatus*) §2. The title *comes* during this period indicates the commander-in-chief of the army in North Africa; *dux* indicates a provincial commander, in this case, subordinate to the *comes*. For a discussion of the changing roles of *comes* and *dux*, see René Cagnat, *L'Armée romaine d'Afrique et l'occupation militaire de l'Afrique sous les empereurs* (Paris: Imprimerie nationale, 1913; repr. New York: Arno, 1975), pp. 713 and 718.

[41] *Cod. Theod.* 9.34.1 (Pharr, p. 249).

[42] Constantine to all the bishops and people of the Catholic Church, preserved in Optatus, Appendix 9 (Vassall-Phillips, pp. 408-409). On the dating, see Frend, *TDC*, p. 161.

[43] Optatus 3.3 (Vassall-Phillips, pp. 131-36).

[44] *The Passion of Donatus* §§3 and 12; *The Passion of Maximian and Isaac* §1.

for a mitigation of his *judicia* (decrees). Members of the committee, all
senior bishops, were treated roughly. One died on the spot and another
was later executed.[45] Still others were exiled.

Eventually, Constans learned the same lesson as his father, i.e., that
Donatism was very deeply rooted and making martyrs or even confessors
was a counterproductive policy. He too relented and recalled his troops.
Donatism and Catholicism returned to their old *modus vivendi*, living side
by side in towns and villages. And so it seems the Highest Divinity was
not moved to wrath either against the human race or against the emperor,
at least not yet. The later history of Donatism included the final round
of persecution under Honorius and Arcadius in the fifth century. The
prudence of the emperor and the sagacity of his Catholic advisors assured
that this persecution would have only civil and economic constraints. So
it produced no stories of martyrs, and, therefore, it falls outside the realm
of this book. But one more issue needs clarification for an accurate reading
of the stories in this volume. That issue is torture.

TORTURE

Considerations of torture in the stories of the martyrs often revolve
around the formalized way in which torture is presented, the literary
commonplaces, and the consequent lack of credibility for the accounts
Reports of torture are highly stylized in the earliest Christian martyr
stories and turn especially gruesome and bloody when the threat of actual
historical persecution is past. What accounts for the treatments of torture
which occur in the stories of this volume? The considerations of this part
of the chapter are designed to help the reader evaluate the reports and their
function in the Christian communities which heard them.

Many readers of this volume live in cultures which, at least publicly,
condemn torture. We take for granted that a defendant is innocent until
proven guilty. We protect accused persons from being forced to give self-
incriminating statements. Torture does not fit our conceptions of humane
treatment, even of the worst members of society. But the populations of
the ancient world had other ideas. So the first considerations must be the

---

[45] *The Martyrdom of Marculus.*

status of torture at the time of the stories of the martyrs and its actual use.

In the Roman empire, torture was a legally sanctioned and socially acceptable part of the judicial process. It could be employed either as a device for ensuring truth in inquiry or as a form of punishment. In general and especially in the case of the stories in this volume, the former was the more important.

According to Roman judicial procedure, torture ensured that the person testifying would tell the truth. Sometimes simply the threat of torture was considered sufficient.[46] Though the information gained from testimony under torture was not in itself probative, it could provide corroboration of other evidence.[47] That it was not probative may be inferred from the fact that persons confessing their own guilt under torture could not accuse others at the same time, hoping they would share in the guilt and the penalty. A separate, better-founded accusation with a trial and additional evidence would be required.[48]

Torture was legally inflicted only on members of the lower classes. In theory, upper classes were exempt, but repeated legislation and the stories of martyrs testify to the breach of this regulation.[49] Children and pregnant women were also exempt. Eventually Christian priests were included in the category of persons who were not to be tortured for information, but as the stories in this volume testify, Donatist priests were not exempt in practice.[50] Even members of the upper class could have their exemptions suspended if they were engaged as tax collectors or accused of especially heinous crimes.[51]

Exactly how were people tortured? The law recognized a variety of

---

[46] Cod. Theod. 4.6.3 (Pharr, p. 86); cf. 2.27.1 (Pharr, p. 58).

[47] *Cod. Theod.* 11.36.1 (Pharr, pp. 334-35).

[48] *Cod. Theod.* 9.1.19 (Pharr, p. 227) and repeatedly in the stories of the martyrs, especially the story of the Abitinians, where individuals are interrogated despite the group admissions made by persons under torture. See the discussion of the adage "You cannot begin with torture" in J. A. Crook, *Law and Life in Rome* (Ithaca: Cornell, 1967), p. 275.

[49] Cf. *The Acts of the Abitinian Martyrs* §§3 and 8; and *Cod. Theod.* 9.35.1-3 and 6 (Pharr, pp. 250-51); and 12.1.39 (Pharr, p. 347).

[50] *Cod. Theod.* 11.39.10 (Pharr, p. 341). But note that whether lower clergy could be tortured or not still depended to some degree on their social class. See *The Acts of the Abitinian Martyrs* §§3 and 11; and *The Martyrdom of Marculus* §§ 1 and 3.

[51] *Cod. Theod.* 8.1.4 and 9.16.6 (Pharr, pp. 186 and 238).

means: whipping with cords, whipping with a lead-tipped scourge, claws used for scraping the sides of a person, and the horse or rack. With the use of the rack, a person lying on a platform had ropes tied to hands and feet. The ropes were pulled gradually using a ratcheted wheel or weights, until the joints of the person's extremities were dislocated and the sockets exposed.[52] Starvation was also common. Martyr stories reveal many other forms of torture such as forcing victims to eat and drink noxious substances, exposing victims to quicklime and fire, and beating with various implements.[53]

In order to keep the cruelty of these means in some perspective, the skeptical reader should read the annual reports of Amnesty International and other twentieth-century accounts of torture. Even a casual perusal of these sources will make ancient Roman torture seem very tame by comparison.

Besides the legal aspects of torture, one must consider the complex nature of torture as a human phenomenon.[54] People torture others for many reasons. The most commonly recognized is the extraction of information, often for self-incrimination. But beyond information used in the conviction of the victim and the implication of the victim's associates, torture has other purposes. It changes conduct: it terrifies members of the victim's community who fear that they themselves might be subject to the same treatment *if they continue the conduct for which the victim was tortured*. But torture continues even when there is no more information to extract and when people are totally terrified, because torture has one more purpose, its most important one. Torture creates a new world, one in which the world construction of the torturers replaces that of the victims *in the minds of the victims themselves*.

So why did Donatists repeat stories of torture? Surely they did not do it to terrify themselves or to deconstruct their own world. The question

---

[52] *Cod. Theod.* 9.35.2 (whips), 8.1.4 and 14.17.6 (horse); 9.16.5 (claws and horse) (Pharr, pp. 251, 186, 418, and 237-38).

[53] Dietary torture in *The Passion of Maxima* §§3 and 5; exposure to quicklime §5, singeing hair §5; beating with switches in *The Passion of Isaac and Maximian* §§5 and 7; and beating with clubs in *The Martyrdom of Marculus* §§4 and 5.

[54] Many of the consideration outlined in this section are more fully explored in my article on torture and the body in hagiography; see note 4 of this chapter.

of the function of the torture scenes in the stories themselves now comes
to the fore. The stories themselves attest their purpose. *The Acts of the
Abitinian Martyrs* is perhaps the most explicit saying: "These [records]
were inscribed in the indispensable archives of memory lest both the
glories of the martyrs and the condemnation of the traitors fade with the
passing of the ages."[55] But *Sermon on the Passion of Saints Donatus and
Advocatus* is no less eloquent as it places blame where it belongs: "Here
in the inscriptions [of the basilica], memory preserves the name of the
persecution as Caecilianist until the end of time, lest after his episcopate
the parricide deceive others who were not privy to the things done in his
name."[56] By keeping alive the memory of the martyrs, the stories accomplished several purposes: they kept alive the sense of the Donatist church
as a church in touch with its roots in the pre-Constantinian persecuted
Christianity; they kept alive animosity for the Catholics who persecuted
them in league with the Roman government; they kept alive traditions on
how to survive physical persecution; they kept alive a heritage of resistance not only to physical force but to the economic and social pressure
to conform to state-sponsored Catholicism. In short, the scenes of torture
served to keep Donatism alive by offering and reinforcing an alternate
construal of reality. It is that construct which the reader is now invited
to experience.

---

[55] *The Acts of the Abitinian Martyrs* §1
[56] *The Passion of Donatus* §8.

THE DONATIST PASSION OF CYPRIAN

INTRODUCTION

Thascius Caecilianus Cyprianus (*ca.* 200-258) was the major theologian and bishop of North African Christianity in the pre-Donatist period. His tenure during the repression under Decius (249-251) and Valerian (253 to Cyprian's death in 258) made him a model for Donatist perseverance in persecution. His strong stance on the unity of the Church, cautious reconciliation of the lapsed, and rejection of the validity of schismatic baptism made his theology especially attractive to the Donatists. His status as martyr was the capstone of his reputation.

The exact date and the author of *The Donatist Passion of Cyprian* are unknown. The *terminus a quo* is obviously the death of Cyprian (September 15, 258), or more accurately, the latter half of the third century since the author presupposes the audience's knowledge of the traditions enshrined in *The Acts of Saint Cyprian* and in Pontius' *The Life and Passion of Cyprian.*[1] The text circulated with a number of pseudo-Cyprianic tracts collected into a unit about the time of the beginning of the Donatist controversy in the early fourth century.[2] This would place the writing between 260 and 314.

The Acts is a more extended version of the events narrated in *The Passion* but often the two stories of the martyrdom are identical for many sentences at a time. There are three major differences among the various accounts of interest to historians.

---

[1] These are available in English: *The Acts* in Musurillo, pp. 168-175, and *The Life and Passion* in ANF 5.267-274.

[2] Richard Reitzenstein, "Ein donatistisches Corpus cyprianischer Schriften," *Nachrichten de königlischen Gesellschaft der Wissenschaften zu Göttingen*, Phil.-hist. Klasse 1914 (pp. 85-92), p. 89. For the other documents, see *S. Thasci Cypriani Opera Omnia*, edited by Gulielmus [William] Hartel, CSEL 3/3 (Vienna: Geroldi, 1871).

The first of the differences concerns Cyprian's dress at his arraignment. In *The Donatist Passion*, the Roman officers disguised him for his transport from his place of exile to his place of judgment. Cyprian's popularity may have made this subterfuge a necessity. While *The Acts* know nothing of this, *The Life and Passion* §16 tells how an ex-Christian officer at the praetorium offered him a change of clothes because Cyprian was wet with perspiration. Either account, disguise or pity, might lie behind Cyprian being arraigned in clothes obviously not his own. However, Pontius's story seems to be decorated at this point with such hagiographic embroidery as to lend credence to the Donatist story of disguise.

The second difference is Cyprian's response to the pronouncement of judgment. Only in *The Donatist Passion* does he respond "Praise God" (*Deo laudes*). Elsewhere one finds the response "Thanks be to God" (*Deo gratias*). While the former phrase has often been characterized as a Donatist war-cry, the evidence up to the fifth century indicates that the phrases are interchangeable.[3]

The third difference concerns the presence of co-martyrs. *The Donatist Passion* indicates that Cyprian was transported alone but was arraigned with others. *The Acts* record that bystanders volunteered for martyrdom once Cyprian's sentence was pronounced (§5.1). Surprisingly, it is the orthodox *Acts* which records this volunteering for martyrdom which is usually attributed to Donatism by its opponents. Both accounts agree then that Cyprian was not martyred alone.

Two additional differences are trivial and stylistic. *The Donatist Passion* stipulates that Cyprian gave his executioners twenty gold pieces; the *Acts* records twenty-five. Finally, at the end of the stories, Galerius Maximus dies a few days after Cyprian, almost as a punishment for the execution of the holy martyr. The Donatist version intimates that he realized the error of his ways before he died and his anguish over his misdeed caused his untimely end.

The translation is based on Theological manuscript 33, folio 38 (9th century) of the Würzburg Library, as reproduced in Maier, pp. 123-26.

---

[3] Hippolyte Delehaye, "Review of Paul Monceaux, *L'epigraphie donatiste*," in *AB* 29 (1910), pp. 467-68.

TRANSLATION

The passion of Cyprian from the day on which the blessed martyr Cyprian underwent his martyrdom. Its sequence is described and explained in this text.

When the holy martyr Cyprian, chosen by the Lord God, returned from the city of Curubis to which he had gone as an exile under the order of Aspasius Paternus who was then proconsul,[4] he remained on his country estate in accord with the imperial rescript[5] granted specifically to him, and he waited through each hour for the day to come just as it had been revealed to him.[6] While he stayed in that place no one looked for him there.

Suddenly on the Ides of September,[7] in the consulate of Tuscus and Bassus, two officers came to him. One was from the office of his excellency Galerius Maximus, the proconsul[8] who succeeded Aspasius Paternus. The other was a knight[9] from among the guards of the office of the same proconsul. They placed Cyprian in a chariot. They both disguised him and they rapidly flew to Sextus' estate where Galerius Maximus had retired to recover his health. His excellency Galerius Maximus the proconsul ordered Cyprian to present himself there on another day, i.e., on the following day. So Cyprian went there with the centurion, i.e., the groom of the office of his excellency Maximus, and he stayed in his town house on Saturn Street between Venus and Health Streets.

All the brothers and sisters[10] remained right there in front of the door, and when Cyprian heard about this, he gave instructions that the young women should be reprimanded because everybody was loitering in the

---

[4] Proconsul in 256/257.

[5] According to *The Acts* §1.4 (Musurillo, p. 169), a rescript of Valerian and Gallienus allowed for his exile to Curubis instead of his execution. Cf. *The Life and Passion* §11 (ANF 5.271).

[6] Pontian's *Life* tells the story of Cyprian's dream in which he learns that he has one year to wait before his death (§§12-13, ANF 5.271-72.)

[7] September 13, 258.

[8] Proconsul 257/258.

[9] *Eques.*

[10] Literally, *universus populus fratruum.*

street in front of the door of the centurion's town house.

On the next day, as I have said, on the eighteenth before the Kalends of October in the consulate of Tuscus and Bassus,[11] Cyprian was brought in right away. His excellency Galerius Maximus the proconsul said, "Are you Thascius Cyprian?"

Cyprian responded, "I am."

His excellency Galerius Maximus said, "Have you represented yourself as bishop for these people with their impious attitude?"

Cyprian answered, "I have."

After speaking with his council, the proconsul pronounced judgment with difficulty, even reluctantly. He said these words: "For quite a while you have lived with an impious attitude and you have gathered around yourself many people in an ungodly company of conspiracy. You have presented yourself as an enemy of the Roman deities and of their holy religion. Even in the security of these most fortunate times, the holy princes, including Valerian, the most noble Caesar, for some time now have not been able to call you back from the idiocy of your persistent madness to celebrating the rites of the Roman people and to maintaining an upright disposition. Since you are the perpetrator of a most wretched crime and a leader discovered in that crime, and because you in your hostility have been unfaithful to the Roman people along with those people whom you have instructed in a wickedness like your own, you will suffer this punishment as an example. In this way, your unholy stubbornness will pay the penalty in your blood."

Cyprian said, "Praise God!" and the believers all together said, "Praise God!"

Then his excellency Galerius Maximus the proconsul read his sentence from the writing tablet: "It is decided that Thascius Cyprian along with his followers shall be punished by the sword."

So he was led from the praetorium to the field of Sextus and a great crowd followed him. There Cyprian folded his cloak, placed it on the ground and knelt on it. Then he took off his dalmatic[12] and handed it to

---

[11] September 14, 258.

[12] The dalmatic was a T-shaped tunic which fell to below the knees. It was ornamented by two stripes running from front to back over the shoulders.

the deacons and stood on this striped linen cloak. Waiting for the executioner, he raised his eyes to heaven in prayer. When the brutal executioner arrived, he lowered his eyes from heaven to the earth and he ordered that twenty gold pieces be given to the executioner. Many handkerchiefs were thrown by the sisters and brothers onto the linen garment on which he was standing.[13]

Then Cyprian began to blindfold himself with his handkerchief. When he could not do it, Julian the presbyter and the subdeacon Donatus tied the handkerchief for him.

Thus Cyprian died along with the others. His body was placed nearby because of the curiosity of the Gentiles[14] and a great crowd followed him. During the night Cyprian's body was carried from the place where he had been laid. Many of the brothers and sisters carrying candles and torches brought it with devotion and great triumph to the property of Macrobius Candidatus the procurator which was on Mappalia Street near the pools. There is where he was buried. Then, a few days later, condemned by his own repentance and consumed by infirmity, his excellency Galerius Maximus the proconsul died.

---

[13] The handkerchiefs would catch Cyprian's blood and become *brandea*, relics of his martyrdom.

[14] I.e., the non-Christians.

THE ACTS OF SAINT FELIX
BISHOP AND MARTYR

INTRODUCTION

Felix of Thibiuca, bishop and martyr, is otherwise unknown. According to *The Acts*, he was caught up in the persecution of Christians which followed the first of the anti-Christian edicts issued under Diocletian at Nicomedia on February 24, 303. While the text of the first edict does not survive, the testimonies of Lactantius and Eusebius indicate that the law commanded that copies of the scriptures were to be burned and church properties both real and moveable were to be confiscated. Christians lost all civil rights including the exemption of *honestiores* from torture. When even this policy, aimed at the more public manifestations of Christianity and the *honestiores,* failed to discourage the Christian movement, the government pursued the rank and file of the movement. Eventually all Christians, not just officials of the Church, were forced to offer sacrifice.[1]

The first edict was promulgated in North Africa on June 5, 303, and Felix was martyred on July 15 for his refusal to hand over the scriptures to be burned.

Neither Felix nor any of the other persons in the story can be identified with great accuracy. The location of Thibiuca is also in doubt. However, R. Duncan-Jones attempts to identify Thibiuca with Henchir Bou Cha through the name of Magnilianus the curator mentioned in the *Acts.* Evidence locates Q. Vetulenius Urbanus Herennianus, known as Magnilianus (as was his son), as a resident of Henchir Bou Cha (a city whose ancient name is unknown). Duncan-Jones's argument is based on the rarity

---

[1] Lactantius, *Of the Manner in which the Persecutors Died* §§12-13 and 15 (ANF 7.305-306); and Eusebius, *EH* 8.2.4-5 (Loeb 2.257-259).

of the name and the fact that both the inquisitor of Felix and Herennianus (Magnilianus senior) were *curatores*. In addition, the town named Thibiuca in antiquity was the same distance from Carthage on ancient itineraries as modern Henchir Bou Cha is from Carthage. The large number of widely variant spellings of Thibiuca in the manuscript tradition lend credibility to his thesis.[2] But aside from the fact that Herennianus was a generous benefactor to his town and *flamen perpetuus*, the story of Felix of Thibiuca, or wherever, receives no additional elucidation.

While this text provides no evidence of having been used specifically by Donatists against Catholics, it does provide background information for the consideration of later stories. First, it makes clear that the essence of being a faithful Christian is guarding the scriptures, even at the cost of one's life. Second, it illustrates more clearly than the other stories procedures for the translation of confessors from small towns to Carthage for arraignment and judgment. In addition, it provides a stylistic bridge between *The Donatist Passion of Cyprian* and the later Donatist stories.

The text used is that of Hippolyte Delehaye, reproduced in both Maier and Musurillo.[3]

TRANSLATION

§1   Under the Augusti Diocletian (consul for the eighth time) and Maximian (consul for the seventh time), an edict of the emperors and caesars went out over the whole face of the earth. It was promulgated in the towns and cities by the officials and magistrates, each in his own area. They were to wrest by force the sacred books from the hands of bishops and presbyters.

---

[2] "An African Saint and his Interrogator," *Journal of Theological Studies* 25/2 (1974), pp. 106-110.

[3] *La Passion de S. Felix de Thibiuca*, AB 39 (1921), pp. 241-276; Maier, pp. 49-56; and Musurillo, pp. 266-70. Musurillo (pp. 270-71) reprints an appendix found in Thierry Ruinart, *Acta primorum Martyrum sincera et selecta* (1689; repr. Ratisbon 1859), pp. 390-91. It details the travels under guard of the bishop to Apulia where he was reputed to have been martyred six weeks after the date of his African martyrdom. Because it is obviously an interpolation designed to justify the cult of Felix in Italy, it offers no light on the Donatist situation in Africa. Thus it is not included in this volume.

On the Nones of June[4] the edict was posted in the city of Thibiuca. At that time Magnilianus the curator[5] ordered the *seniores* of the people[6] to be brought to him. (On that same day Felix the bishop [of Thibiuca] left for Carthage.) Magnilianus ordered Aper the presbyter and Cyril and Vitalis the lectors to be brought to him.[7]

§2   Magnilianus the curator said to them, "Do you have the sacred books?"

Aper said, "We do."

Magnilianus the curator said, "Turn them over to be burnt in the fire."

Then Aper said, "Our bishop has them with him."

Magnilianus the curator said, "Where is he?"

Aper said, "I don't know."

Magnilianus the curator said, "Then you will remain in custody until you render an account to Anulinus the proconsul."[8]

§3   The next day, however, Felix the bishop arrived at Thibiuca from Carthage and Magnilianus the curator ordered him to be brought in by an officer. Magnilianus said to him, "Are you Felix the bishop?"

Felix answered, "I am."

Magnilianus the curator said, "Turn over whatever books or parchments you have."[9]

Felix the bishop said, "I have them but I won't turn them over."

Magnilianus the curator said, "Turn over the books so they can be burned."

Felix the bishop said, "It is better for me to be burned in the fire than

---

[4] June 5th, 303.

[5] The title *curator* was given to a variety of administrative officials.

[6] The fiscal responsibilities of North African churches were in the hands of a collegial body called the *seniores*. On their responsibilities, see W. H. C. Frend, "The Seniores Laici and the Origins of the Church in North Africa," *Journal of Theological Studies* n.s. 12 (1961), pp. 280-84.

[7] Felix and the other Christians in this story are otherwise unknown.

[8] C. Annius Anulinus was proconsul at Carthage in 303-304/305. His name is spelled variously (including Anolinus), but the spelling of *The Acts of Saint Felix* is the most common in Christian literature and will be used throughout this volume.

[9] Books or parchments—The Scriptures and lectionaries were not necessarily bound as a single volume. Obedience to the edict might mean that the authorities of a single congregation might hand over many volumes and even individual pages.

the sacred scriptures, because it is better to obey God than any human authority (Acts 5.29)."

Magnilianus the curator said, "What the emperor ordered takes priority over what you say."

Felix the bishop said, "The Lord's command takes priority over human authority."

Magnilianus the curator said, "Think it over for three days, because if you fail to obey what was commanded in this city, you will go before the proconsul and you will continue this conversation in his court."

§4   Then, after three days, the curator ordered Felix the bishop to be brought to him and he said to him, "Have you thought it over?"

Felix the bishop said, "What I said before I am saying now and I will say before the proconsul."

Magnilianus the curator said, "Then you will go to the proconsul and you will render an account there." Then Vincentius Celsinus, a decurion[10] of the city of Thibiuca, was assigned to him as an escort.

§5   So Felix the bishop set out from Thibiuca to Carthage on the eighteenth day before the Kalends of July.[11] When he had arrived, he was presented to the legate[12] who ordered him to be thrown into prison. The next day, however, Felix the bishop was brought out before dawn. The legate said to him, "Why don't you hand over your useless scriptures?"

Felix the bishop said, "I have them but I will not turn them over." So the legate ordered him to be sent into the lowest reaches of the prison.[13]

After sixteen days Felix the bishop was brought out in chains to Anul-

---

[10] A decurion was a member of the town council or *curia*. Under the empire the decurions were responsible for the orderly functioning of urban services, including collection of the taxes in their city.

[11] June 14th.

[12] The legate was an assistant to the provincial governor. Occasionally, this officer would be deputed to hear legal cases.

[13] Prisons often had many levels below ground with the most secure cells at the lowest level. An accessible example is the Mamertine prison near the Forum in Rome with two levels below ground. As one descends, the stairways linking the levels grow progressively narrower, making security easier to maintain. If the water table is high, the cells also grow more humid as one descends.

inus the proconsul at the fourth hour of the night.[14] Anulinus the proconsul said to him, "Why don't you give up your useless scriptures?"

Felix the bishop responded, "I cannot give them up." At that point Anulinus the proconsul ordered him to be executed by the sword on the Ides of July.[15]

Felix the bishop, raising his eyes to heaven, said with a loud voice, "Thank you, God. I have been in this world for fifty-six years. I have guarded my virginity; I have served the gospel; and I have preached the truth. Lord God of heaven and earth, Jesus Christ, I bend my neck to you as a sacrificial victim, you who remain forever."[16]

When he finished speaking, he was led off by soldiers and beheaded. He was buried in [the Basilica] Fausti on the road called Scillitan.[17]

---

[14] Ten o'clock in the evening.

[15] July 15th.

[16] Cf. a similar statement in the model *Martyrdom of Polycarp* §9.6 (Musurillo, p. 9).

[17] This indicates the final resting place of the bishop. The road was named for a nearby town whose location is now unknown. For a discussion of possible locations, see *Actes de la Conférence de Carthage*, 4.1456-1457. It was from Scilli that the first North African martyrs came. See their story, *The Acts of the Scillitan Martyrs*, in Musurillo, pp. 86-89.

THE PASSION OF SAINTS MAXIMA, DONATILLA AND SECUNDA

INTRODUCTION

Very little is known about Saints Maxima, Donatilla, and Secunda other than the story of their interrogations and beheading. The execution of the saints is dated to July 30, from internal evidence (three days before the Kalends of August) in the *titulus* and from the traditional feast day in the Calendar of Carthage and in the martyrologies of Jerome and Ado.

The year of the martyrdom presents more of a problem. According to the titulus the martyrs died under Maximian, with Anulinus as proconsul. Maximian was emperor from 286 until he resigned on May 1, 305. But the body of the text (§1 *bis*) maintains that Maximian was reigning with Gallienus (259-68). This error is perhaps the confusion of the persecution of Christians under Valerian (who was succeeded by Gallienus) and the later persecution under Maximian. More likely, this is really a reference to Galerius, not Gallienus, since Galerius was *caesar* under Maximian. The persecution of the laity began early in the summer of 303 giving a *terminus a quo*. The execution of these martyrs is attested in some manuscripts of *The Martyrdom of Crispina*.[1] Crispina's execution on December 5, 304, provides a *terminus ante quem*. The final piece of evidence furnishes the necessary precision to date the execution. Maxima, Donatilla and Secunda were executed under the provisions of the fourth edict of Diocletian promulgated in the spring of 304. It required that all Christians, not only ecclesiastical leaders, offer sacrifice to the gods.[2] Thus the execution of Maxima, Secunda, and Donatilla must be dated to

---

[1] Musurillo, pp. 302-209.

[2] For a succinct account of the evidence for the promulgation of the edict, see W. H. C. Frend, *The Rise of Christianity* (Philadelphia: Fortress, 1984), p. 461.

July 30, 304.

Dating the writing of the narrative itself is another task. Obviously July 30, 304 is the *terminus a quo*. The story provides an additional clue which indicates an early date for the original story. According to the narrator, the saints were interred at a place for mass burials of victims of the beasts.[3] The narrator records the inability of the Christian community to obtain their remains, even at the time of the writing (§6). This probably indicates a very early date for the account, probably before the end of the persecution.[4]

Dating the final form is more difficult, but evidence leads to at least a second edition. Paul Monceaux and Hippolyte Delehaye take the parts of the story about Secunda as interpolations. She appears late in the story and is not associated with the condemnations of the other two young women.[5] When these sections might have been added is unknown, but both authors see them as useful to later Donatist propaganda in their advocacy of voluntary martyrdom, and especially in Secunda's self-defenestration.[6] Even Secunda's name seems to have been an afterthought since it appears only in the latter parts of the story, and then, as "Maxima *and* Donatilla *and* Secunda."[7] Epigraphical evidence (CIL VIII 14902), though undated, also suggests the later addition of Secunda.

---

[3] See Charles de Smedt's comments on the martyrdom, p. 116, n. 21.

[4] Monceaux, 3.150-51, dates the final edition of the story to the early fifth century to make it especially useful as Donatist propaganda. His evidence is based on vocabulary: *paganus* (§1) and *quievit in pace* (§6). Pio Franchi de'Cavalieri, "Della 'Passio sanctarum Maximae, Donatillae et Secundae,'" in *Note Agiografiche VIII* in *Studi e Testi* 65 (1935), p. 76, follows Monceaux. Their evidence is weak, for *paganus* is already used in the sense of this story by the end of the second century. See Tertullian, *De corona* 11.4-5 in *Quintii Septimi Florentis Tertulliani Opera Omnia*, edited by E. Dekkers, CCSL 1 and 2 (Turnhout: Brepols, 1953), p. 2.1057. The word is strangely invisible in the ANF 3.100 translation. Monceaux dates the use of *quievit in pace* for 'death' to the fifth century on the basis of CIL VIII 8644; however, *quiesco* as an expression for the sleep of the dead is found as early as the first century BCE in Vergil, *Aeneid* 1.249.

[5] Monceaux, 3.150; cf. H. Delehaye, "Contributions récentes à l'hagiographie de Rome et d'Afrique," *AB* 54 (1936), pp. 298-300.

[6] Franchi de'Cavalieri (p. 87) takes this precipitation as her martyrdom. For a similar story, see *The Acts of the Abitinian Martyrs* §17, n. 47.

[7] Maier, p. 110.

The three young women are modelled on Shadrach, Meschach and Abednego in the Book of Daniel. Theirs is the story of stalwart youths bravely standing against imperial authority even when their religious elders and authorities failed to remain faithful to their ancestral religion. The three North Africans whose youth is deliberately highlighted (§2) remained faithful when all others, including Catholic priests, did not. Such a story would have been extremely useful to Donatists when many of the Catholic clergy collaborated with the idolatrous (in their eyes) Roman Empire. There are no other contemporary records indicating a mass apostasy of North African Christians as described in this passion. According to Cyprian, a significant number of Christians did comply with the imperial edict to sacrifice in Carthage fifty years earlier, but the scene in §1 seems to have been deliberately drawn to emphasize the similarities of the heroines to the youths in the book of Daniel.[8]

The women are also modelled on Jesus. This literary tactic of assimilating the passion of martyrs to the sufferings of Jesus begins as early as the narrative of the martyrdoms of Stephen and Polycarp. Stephen's story (Acts 6.8-8.1) has a charge of blasphemy similar to that against Jesus (6.11) and final words similar to his: "Lord, Jesus, receive my spirit" and "Lord, do not hold this sin against them" (7.59-60). But Polycarp's story is much more conformed to that of Jesus. It opens with an explicit reference to the imitative behavior: "Just as the Lord did, he too waited that he might be delivered up, that we might become his imitators, *not thinking of ourselves alone, but of our neighbors as well.*"[9] Polycarp like Jesus received premonitions of his sufferings while in prayer and prayed that God's will be done.[10] He was betrayed by intimates, slaves of his household, who in the end suffer the same way as Judas.[11] Polycarp and Jesus suffer on a Friday before a major Sabbath.[12] Polycarp enters the town on a donkey as Jesus too had done.[13]

---

[8] See Cyprian, *On the Lapsed* 7-8 (ANF 5.438-439).

[9] See *The Martyrdom of Saint Polycarp* §1 quoting Phil. 2.4, in Musurillo, pp. 2-21, specifically, p. 3.

[10] *Polycarp* §§5 and 7 (Musurillo, pp. 5-7).

[11] *Polycarp* §6 (Musurillo, p. 7).

[12] *Polycarp* §§7 and 8 (Musurillo, pp. 7-9).

[13] *Polycarp* §8 (Musurillo, p. 9).

Between Polycarp and Maxima, North African martyr stories owe a major debt to their shaping by *The Passion of Perpetua and Felicity*;[14] however, for this story Jesus, directly and perhaps through Polycarp, provides a model for martyrdom.

In *The Martyrdom of Polycarp* we find the first evidence that Christians were tortured by being made to lie on a bed of crushed shells, just as these young women would be.[15]

In the case of Maxima, Donatilla and Secunda, the language of Jesus' passion provides words and phrases for their story, from betrayal by an associate and the abjuration of Anulinus in the language of the high priest at Jesus' trial (§2) to being forced to drink gall and vinegar (§3) and to rejoicing in the approach of their hour of glory (§6).

While the interrogation of the martyrs has some elements of the Jesus tradition, one oddity is the conversation regarding magic and occult (§2). Initially it appears quite out of place in a story of Christian martyrdom. Maier, in fact, takes it to be *une grossière interpolation*.[16] It is true that the interrogation would make better sense if the question on age were immediately followed by the answer (which is delayed by this dialogue on sorcery). But the exchange between Anulinus and Maxima is not out of character for the period or for the rest of the story. The charges they hurl at one another are comprehensible in their context. Christians accused Roman authorities of being in league with the devil simply because the Romans were persecuting them. Romans accused Christians of practicing magic if any remained steadfast under torture; it was believed that one might anoint one's body with some special ointment and thereby be

---

[14] *The Passion of Perpetua and Felicitas* (Musurillo, pp. 106-131) provides motifs, especially dream material for *The Martyrdom of Marian and James* (Musurillo, pp. 194-213), and *The Martyrdom of Montanus and Lucius* (Musurillo, pp. 214-239) and the later *Martyrdom of Marculus*. See the discussion of their relationship in Cées Martyns, "Les premiers martyrs et leurs rêves: cohésion de l'histoire and des rêves dans quelques 'passions' latins de l'Afrique du Nord," *Revue d'histoire ecclésiastique* 81/1-2 (1986), pp. 5-46; and Michel Meslin, "Vases sacrés et boissons d'éternité dans les visions des martyrs africains," in *Epektasis: Mélanges patristiques offerts au Cardinal Jean Daniélou*, edited by Jacques Fontaine and Charles Kannengiesser (Paris: Beauchesne, 1972).

[15] *Polycarp* §3 (Musurillo, p. 5) and *The Passion of Maxima* §5.

[16] Maier, p. 97, n. 33.

immune to the pain of torture.[17]

The passion of these martyrs also participates in the larger Christian and non-Christian attitude toward the relationship between holy persons and animals, always a positive, helpful one. Two points ought to be considered here. The first is that Donatilla understood the speech of the bear who was to execute the martyrs. Only those who were exceptionally pure of heart participated in the Edenic rapport with the animals. Second, the bear appeared to have some hesitancy about being the agent of Maxima's execution. Donatilla tried to relieve the bear of his guilt by saying, "Do what is commanded of you; don't be afraid." But the bear took the initiative in its refusal to participate in the martyrdom, a common theme in martyr stories. Instead, it licked the feet of the martyrs and left the young women unharmed. The act of licking was essential to the bear's identification of their holiness, for bears often investigate their surroundings through their sense of taste. Once the bear had tasted the ground where they trod, it could not participate in their slaughter for it knew them to be saintly.[18]

This translation is based on the one surviving manuscript of the story, edited by Charles De Smedt in *Analecta Bollandiana* 9 (1890) 107-116, and reproduced in Maier, pp. 92-105.

TRANSLATION

The passion of the holy virgins Maxima and Secunda and Donatilla who suffered under the emperor Maximian and the proconsul Anulinus three days before the Kalends of August.

§1 In those days Maximian and Gallienus the emperors sent letters through the entire province that the Christians should sacrifice on the

---

[17] Such were the charges brought by Romans against Rabbi Akiba (*ca.* 50-*ca.* 135). See Louis Finkelstein, *Akiba: Scholar, Saint and Martyr*, (New York: Covici, Friede, 1936; repr. Northvale, NJ, and London: Jason Aronson, 1990), p. 276.

[18] For an extended discussion of the interaction between animals and holy persons, see Maureen A. Tilley, "Martyrs, Monks, Insects and Animals," in *The Medieval World of Nature: A Book of Essays*, edited by Joyce E. Salisbury (New York and London: Garland, 1993), pp. 93-107.

Cephalitan estate.[19] Anulinus the proconsul entered precisely at the evening hour. Rising at the sixth hour of the night, he called a certain decurion to bring in Modaticius and Archadius the magistrates.[20] When they had come, they were ordered by the proconsul to bring in all the Christians. They immediately sent members of their staff to arraign the Christians.[21] And about the third hour of the day[22] when the proconsul had taken his seat on the tribunal, all the Christians on this estate gathered together. And with all of them standing there, Anulinus the proconsul said: "Are you Christians or pagans?"[23]

They all said, "We are Christians."

Anulinus the proconsul said: "Maximian and Gallienus, the godfearing and august emperors, deigned to deliver letters to me that all Christians should come and sacrifice; however, any who would refuse and would not obey their commands should be punished with various torments and tortures." Then they all feared greatly for themselves and their spouses, and even the young men and women were afraid. Among them were even presbyters and deacons with all ranks of the clergy. Throwing themselves on the ground they all worshipped the cursed idols (cf. Dan 3.7).

§2   However, there were there two beautiful consecrated virgins,[24] Maxima and Donatilla. Campitana began to shout saying: "We all came

---

[19] The Cephalitan estate cannot be located with precision, but if the Thuburbo referred to in §3 is Thuburbo Maius, the estate may be imperial.

[20] The time is about midnight and these persons are otherwise unknown.

[21] *Officiales privatos*, i.e., assistants whose duties are to arrest and arraign defendants in criminal cases and to execute judgment.

[22] About nine o'clock.

[23] The word used is *pagani*. In the sense of the sentence, it means a practitioner of traditional religions of the Roman Empire, as opposed to a Christian. Non-Christians do not call themselves pagans as a religious term—for them it would mean a 'rustic' or 'peasant'; but the word does have that currency among early fourth-century Christians. The common form of interrogation would have been "Are you a Christian *or not?*"

[24] The young women are called *castimonialae* in this text. The term *sanctimoniales* is also used interchangeably to describe the same class of women. They have taken vows of chastity but are not confined to cloister or to exclusive dedication to the service of the Church. However, there is fourth-century evidence for some sort of ceremony in which their heads were anointed and they were given a veil. See Optatus 2.19 and 6.4 (Vassall-Phillips, pp. 101 and 257) and the Council of Carthage (390) §3 in *Concilia Africae A. 345 - A. 525*, edited by C. Munier, CCSL 149 (Turnhout: Brepols, 1974), p. 13.

to adore the gods and here are these two virgins who have not obeyed the command of the emperors and will not sacrifice."[25]

Anulinus the proconsul said, "Tell me their names."

Campitana said: "They are called Maxima and Donatilla."

Anulinus the proconsul ordered a member of the proconsular staff to bring them out. When they had been led out and were standing there, they said: "Look, here we are. What question do you propose to ask us?"

Anulinus said: "Who authorized you to defy the god-fearing and august emperors?"

Maxima responded: "I am authorized by the Christian faith which I practice."

Anulinus the proconsul said: "How old are you?"[26]

Maxima responded: "So am I the daughter of a magus, the way you are a magus?"[27]

Anulinus the proconsul said: "How would you know whether I am a magus?"

Maxima responded: "Because the Holy Spirit is in us but an evil spirit manifests itself in you."

Anulinus the proconsul said: "By the living God, I adjure you to tell me how old you are (cf. Mt 26.63)."

Maxima responded, "Haven't I told you that you are a magus?"

Anulinus said, "Reveal to me how old you are if you know."

Maxima responded. "May your limbs be broken.[28] I am fourteen years old."

Anulinus the proconsul said, "Today you will finish off [those fourteen

---

[25] The identity of Campitana is unknown. It may be a proper name, but according to de Smedt (*AB* 9.112), it probably reflects a general name for rustics.

[26] The discernment of the age of the accused was of grave importance, especially in capital crimes. The traditions of Roman law proclaimed many circumstances mitigating guilt, including both age and sex. For a succinct discussion of the various conditions, see Giuseppe Carnazza-Rametta, *Studio sul diritto penale dei Romani* (Messina, 1893; repr. Rome: "L'Erma" di Bretschneider, 1972), pp. 115-139, especially 116-119 on age. Maxima's later response that she is fourteen years old places her beyond the legal age, i.e., subject to capital punishment. See n. 33 below.

[27] In this case, *magus* indicates a person who practices sorcery.

[28] Homonymous with "May the walls of your dwelling be broken."

years] if you have not sacrificed to the gods."

Maxima responded, "You sacrifice to them. You are like them."

Anulinus said, "Your verdict is about to be pronounced."

Maxima responded, "Greatly do I desire and wish it."

Anulinus said, "Then prepare yourself for the verdict."

Maxima responded, "It is better for me to receive a verdict from you than to defy the one and true God (cf. Acts 5.29)."

Anulinus said: "How is it that you despair? Will you sacrifice or not?"

Maxima responded: "I stand firm in my God; and I will not worship other gods (2 Kgs 17.35 and 1 Pet 1.25 quoting Isa 40.7-8)."

Anulinus said, "I will be patient with you until you make up your mind."

Maxima responded: "I have made up my mind, and the Lord is fortifying me against you: thus you will grow weak but I will grow strong."

§3   Anulinus said, "Who is with you?"

Maxima responded: "Donatilla, my sister."

Anulinus said, "Donatilla, are you Christian or pagan?"

Donatilla responded, "Still the demon stands firm in you. You are being put to the test by it but you will not be able to put others to the test."

Anulinus said, "Do you stand firm in this same desire?"

Donatilla responded, "Our authority is Christ; your authority is the devil. Between God and the devil there is a great distance (cf. 2 Cor 6.15). Through us God is blessed; through you the devil is cursed."

Anulinus said: "Both of you, sacrifice. For it is good to fear [the gods] and to obey the command of our lords."

Donatilla responded: "The command of the emperor will perish, but the command of the Lord will remain forever (1 Pet 1.25 quoting Isa 40.9; cf. Lev 10.9 and 23.14)."

Anulinus said, "Consider your situation, young lady, lest you suffer torture."

Donatilla responded, "Your tortures will be very useful to my soul."

That day Anulinus put off the case and ordered them to be brought to the city of Turbitan;[29] he also ordered that they consume neither water

---

[29] *Civitatem Turbitanam*, i.e., Thuburbo.

nor bread.[30] Maxima and Donatilla responded: "We have the food of the Most High;[31] you, however, have the food of the devil."

Anulinus said: "Give them gall and vinegar, and let them eat and drink them (Mt 27.34 and 48)."

Maxima and Donatilla responded: "Rather save the vinegar and gall for yourself, and may vinegar preserve you forever." Anulinus then raged in anger and ordered them to go to Turbo.[32]

§4   While they were getting up and going, there was in that place a certain girl by the name of Secunda, about twelve years old, who had been engaged many times and rejected them all because she loved God alone.[33] When she saw them setting out, looking down through the balcony of her house so high, she threw herself down from there, having no consideration for her parents' wealth before her eyes: she disdained all the squalor, as it were, of this world. She despised wealth; only one did she desire, the One she deserved to find in eternity.[34] Therefore, with Maxima and Donatilla on their way to Turbo,[35] Secunda cried out:

---

[30] Starvation was used as a method of torture before interrogation.

[31] For precedents of divine provision of literal or figurative food, see Elijah and the raven in 1 Kgs 17, Jn 4.33-34, and *The Martyrdom of Saints Montanus and Lucius* §9.2 (Musurillo, p. 220).

[32] Though the text has Turbo here and in §4, the previous reference to the Turbitan city in §3 suggests that Turbo is an abbreviation.

[33] The virgin as bride of Christ is found in North African literature as early as 203 in *The Martyrdom of Perpetua and Felicitas* §18.2 (Musurillo, p. 127). Secunda's age of twelve makes her old enough for marriage. Females were considered pubescent and, therefore, old enough for marriage at twelve. Males were considered pubescent at fourteen. See *The Institutes of Gaius* 1.196, edited and translated with a commentary by Francis De Zulueta, 2 vols. (Oxford: Clarendon, 1946 and 1953), p. 63; cf. 2.31; and *Cod. Theod.* 2.17.1 (Pharr, p. 51). Secunda's ability to reject betrothals was based on the fact that, under Roman law, the consent of the woman and the man marrying made them married. Specific dowry or ceremonies or the consent of others was not formally required. See the discussion of consent in De Zulueta, 2.31-32. Gifts given during the betrothal period were normally not recoverable unless they had been publicly recorded and given under the condition that the marriage take place. For a general survey on women in antiquity, see Gillian Clark, *Women in Late Antiquity: Pagan and Christian Lifestyles* (Oxford: Clarendon, 1993), especially the section on marriage, pp. 13-17.

[34] Cf. Victoria in the *Acts of the Abitinian Martyrs* §17, especially n. 47.

[35] See note 32 above.

"Sisters, do not abandon me."

Maxima and Donatilla said to her, "Go away, for you are the only child of your father: to whom would you leave him?"

But Secunda said, "It is better for me to defy my father according to the flesh and to love my spiritual Father."

Maxima and Donatilla said to her: "Consider the age of your father, and do not abandon him."

Secunda said, "God will repay you, if you leave me."

Maxima responded: "Know that a verdict has been prepared for us. Will you be able to endure it?"

Saint Secunda said, "The verdict of this world cannot deter me, because I seek a spiritual spouse, Jesus Christ."

Maxima responded: "People nowadays are weak."

Secunda said: "But I desire to take a spouse who does not corrupt virginity. Oh, such a spouse is he who consoles and comforts the lowliest."

Donatilla responded: "Well, let's go, girl. The day of our passion hurries us along and the angel of blessing comes to meet us along the way." So they left that place, and the sun set.

§5   And afterwards when Maxima and Donatilla and Secunda came again into the city of Thuburbo, five days before the Kalends of August, about the ninth hour,[36] Anulinus, the proconsul ascended the tribunal and he ordered Maxima and Donatilla to be brought in for the verdict. And when they were brought in, Anulinus said: "Will you sacrifice in this city or not?"

Maxima responded: "We are already offering sacrifice to the one to whom we have promised our souls."

The proconsul again on that same day deferred sentencing. But on the next day, i.e., the fourth day before the Kalends of August, at the first hour,[37] Anulinus ascended the tribunal and he ordered Maxima and Donatilla to be lashed thoroughly.[38] Then Maxima said, "The lashes are

---

[36] About mid-afternoon on July 28th.

[37] Shortly after dawn on August 29th.

[38] The use of the lash (*plaga*) is the subject for punning, because when it is of no avail, Anulinus orders the young women to be tortured on beds (*plagas*) of crushed shells.

not heavy when the flesh is flogged and the spirit is saved and the soul
is redeemed and strengthened."

But Anulinus, seeing his punishments performed to no avail, ordered
beds of [crushed] shells and lime prepared and he ordered them to be
placed thereon. Maxima and Donatilla responded: "We have a great
physician who cures the blows you inflict on us and he strengthens our
souls. You are the one diminished in the punishment and we grow in
glory. You are degraded in the verdict and we are strengthened by our
trust in God." Then the proconsul ordered them to be placed on the rack.
But Maxima and Donatilla said: "It is in accord with the judgment of God
that a person should suffer for the master."

Anulinus said, "Now if their throats grow weary and dry out, give them
tatiba to drink."[39]

Maxima and Donatilla said, "You really are a fool.[40] We will have God
most high as our seasoning, won't we?"

The proconsul said, "Sprinkle burning coals on the hair of the heads
of Maxima and Donatilla."

Maxima and Donatilla responded: "What is written in the Law is
true:[41] we have passed through fire and water and we have arrived at
a place of cool refreshment (Ps 66.12)."

§6   Then Anulinus ordered Maxima and Donatilla to be placed in the
amphitheater. Maxima and Donatilla said: "Now the hour approaches us;
pass the sentence you wish."[42]

The proconsul said: "Leave me now, for I am worn out now."

Maxima and Donatilla said: "How can you be worn out after one hour?

---

[39] There is a word play on "throats" (*fauces*) and "grow weary" (*defecerunt*) as well as
the irony that it will be Anulinus himself who will be worn out (*iam deficio*) before the young
women (§6). *Tatiba* appears nowhere else in martyrological or medical literature. De Smedt
suggests that *tatiba* was a highly seasoned liquid which would refresh victims of torture and
allow them to continue in the interrogation (*AB* 9.115). Hermann Stadler's etymology in
PW 6/1.689 leaves open the possibility of relating it to 'vinegar' ("Essig"), the preservative
mentioned in §3.

[40] Continuing the irony, the proconsul is *fatuus*, a word meaning both stupid and insipid,
like food without any seasoning.

[41] The Bible is regularly referred to as "Law" in North Africa.

[42] Language of "the hour" continues the identification of the three young women with Jesus.
Cf. Matt 26.45 and Jn 7.30, 12.23, 17.1, *etc.*

You have just arrived and you are already exhausted."

Anulinus said, "We command Maxima and Donatilla and Secunda to be subjected to torture. We order Maxima and Donatilla and Secunda to fight the beasts."

They said, "The hour is near: do what you want to do." Then the proconsul ordered Fortunatus the animal keeper to bring to him a ferocious bear which he had, which had not eaten in two or three days, and to let it out so that it might devour these young women. They responded, "In the name of our Lord Jesus Christ, we shall overcome you today." And in that same hour Fortunatus the animal keeper let out the ferocious bear. Before it had approached the holy Maxima, Donatilla began to say to it, "Do what was commanded of you; don't be afraid." And immediately the bear roared and Donatilla understood its roar; and the beast licked her feet and sent the virgins of God away unharmed.[43]

Then Anulinus the proconsul announced the verdict from his writing tablet:[44] "We command that Maxima and Donatilla and Secunda be executed by the sword."

They responded: "Thanks be to God," and immediately they suffered. But their bodies were buried in the amphitheater in the place for the bodies of the executed, where they rested in peace, with our Lord Jesus Christ reigning, who lives with God the Father and reigns with the Holy Spirit forever and ever. Amen.

---

[43] The fostering attitude of wild animals toward the truly innocent is a commonplace in antiquity in both Christian and non-Christian literature, e.g., *The Acts of Paul* 7 and 26 where lions refuse to attack Paul and Thecla, in Edgar Hennecke, *New Testament Apocrypha*, edited by Wilhelm Schneemelcher; English translation by R. McL. Wilson, 2 vols. (Philadelphia: Westminster, 1962), 2.360 and 372.

[44] See the formulaic statement also in *The Acts of Cyprian* §2.3 (Musurillo, p. 168) and Pontius' *Vita Caecilii Cypriani* §12 (*CSEL* 3/3.ciii).

THE ACTS OF THE ABITINIAN MARTYRS

INTRODUCTION

The Passion of Saints Dativus, Saturninus the presbyter, et al., also known as *The Acts of the Abitinian Martyrs*, provides insight into the critical period immediately preceding the formal split between Donatists and Catholics. It deals with an incident occurring in 304 involving the Carthaginian bishop Mensurius (d. 311/12) who was later charged with being a *traditor* and his deacon Caecilian who succeeded him in the episcopate. In 304 Roman authorities were enforcing the edict mentioned in *The Passion of Saints Maxima, Donatilla and Secunda* §1 and consequently soldiers arrested a group of Christians in Abitina, a village near Carthage, who were caught in the performance of the liturgy. Because there was no appropriate civil authority in residence in the village, they were transferred to Carthage for their trials under Anulinus.[1]

While they were incarcerated, a remarkable incident took place outside the entrance to their jail. The Carthaginian bishop and his deacon had placed their own guards at the gates of the prison to prevent supporters of the Abitinians from entering with food and other supplies for the imprisoned confessors. These ecclesiastical guards obstructed the path of the Abitinian supporters and a melee ensued.

The author of *The Acts* represented the bishop and deacon as simply hostile to these witnesses to the faith. The writer never mentions the existence of a contemporary law promulgated by Licinius. It prohibited feeding those condemned to starvation in prison (usually as a form of torture). According to Eusebius, the penalty for the perpetrator was a

---

[1] See the introductory comments on *The Acts of Saint Felix Bishop and Martyr*, n. 1, for the identity of Anulinus.

similar death by starvation.[2] It was possible that the bishop and deacon, by respecting that law and attempting to prevent prison visitations, were trying to preserve the rest of the Christian community from arrest. Whether this law, which was repealed in 324 by Constantine, was at the heart of the issue or not is not known.[3] Nonetheless, the writer of the preamble and the epilogue to the story of the Abitinians saw nothing redeeming about the bishop and his deacon interfering with support for the confessors. The epilogue records a letter from the imprisoned Christians excommunicating those who associated with the evil bishop and his deacon. The writer affirms the inspiration of the martyrs by the Holy Spirit and underlines the biblical authority of the excommunication.

The Acts (actually a hybrid of *acta*, *passio*, and letter) were written close in time to the events they narrated. Their compilation, including an added preface and epilogue, date from the period before Caecilian's election as bishop in late 311 or early 312.[4]

Because of the attack on Mensurius for his lack of care for the martyrs and on Caecilian who later led the Catholic community against the Donatists, the *Acts* became a favorite among Donatists, although these martyrs were also venerated among Catholics.[5]

Their story survives in six manuscripts which support two different stories, a Donatist version and a later Catholic account.[6] Migne reproduces two versions. The first is based on that of Étienne Baluze (PL

---

[2] Eusebius, EH 10.8.11 (Loeb 2.471).

[3] For the repeal, see *Cod. Theod.* 15.14.1 (Pharr, p. 437).

[4] This judgment presumes that the treatment of Caecilian as still a deacon is not an archaizing subterfuge of the editor. Considering the remainder of the story, especially the prologue, reference to Caecilian as bishop would have generated a much more potent polemical effect. Hence, we conclude that the Acts were written before his election as bishop.

[5] For evidence of its use by Catholics, see Augustine, *Breviculus Collationis cum Donatistis* 3.17.32 (CSEL 53.81); and Victor Saxer, *Morts, martyrs, reliques en Afrique chrétienne aux premieres siècles: Les témoignages de Tertullien, Cyprien et Augustin à la lumière de l'archéologie africaine*, Théologie historique 55 (Paris: Beauchesne, 1980), pp. 226-27 and 321.

[6] Pio Franchi de'Cavalieri produced an edition which was based primarily on the Catholic version and several minor manuscripts. See *Passio ss. Dativi Presb. et Aliorum* in *Studi e Testi* 65 (1935), introduction pp. 1-46, text pp. 47-71. His edition, by excluding manuscripts which represent Donatist traditions, obscures the Donatist viewpoint.

8.688-703), and the second based that of Thierry Ruinart (PL 8.703-715). Baluze (1630-1718) and Ruinart (1657-1709) were French patristic scholars. In general, Baluze is more sympathetic to these Donatist martyrs though not as much as one of the surviving manuscripts, Bibliothèque National Latin Ms. 5297. Ruinart's version shows some tendencies to discount the heroism of the Abitinians. This chapter uses the Donatist version of the story based on BN Lat. 5297. Significant differences from the versions printed in Migne are listed in the footnotes.

TRANSLATION

Here begin the confessions and the judicial record of the martyrs, Saturninus the presbyter, Dativus, Felix, Ampelius, and the others written below. They confessed the Lord under Anulinus, then proconsul of Africa, on the fifteenth before the Kalends of February,[7] on charges regarding assembly[8] and the scriptures of the Lord; and, in diverse places and at various times, they poured out their most blessed blood.

§1   Everyone endowed with reverence for the most holy faith exults and glories in Christ (cf. Gal 6.14). Once error has been condemned, let whoever rejoices in the Lord's truth read the records of the martyrs so as to hold fast to the Catholic Church and distinguish the holy communion from the unholy. These [records] were inscribed in the indispensable archives of memory lest both the glory of the martyrs and the condemnation of the traitors[9] fade with the passing of the ages. Therefore, I begin an account of celestial battles and struggles undertaken anew by the bravest soldiers of Christ (cf. 2 Cor 10.2), the unconquered warriors, the glorious

---

[7] Neither of the versions reproduced in Migne contains a specific date. This date would be the 17th of January. Another manuscript has the day before the Ides, i.e., the 12th of February.

[8] I.e., liturgical assembly. *Collecta* is the word used consistently in the *Acts*. It indicates the Donatist self-identification with the assembly of Israel (Lev 23.36, Deut 16.8, 2 Chr 7.9, and Neh 8.18). While it is used by Christians outside North Africa, Catholics in North Africa shun its use once Donatists begin to use it.

[9] The term 'traitor' (*traditor*) is etymologically linked to the verb 'to hand over' (*tradere*). It is applied to a person who cooperated with Roman authorities in handing over the scriptures to the Roman authorities. See the discussion of the word in the Preface.

martyrs. I want to emphasize that I begin to write [my account] using public records. I am endowed not so much with any talent as I am joined to them by the respect of a fellow-citizen. I write with a specific two-fold resolve: that we might prepare our very selves for martyrdom by imitating them and that, when we have committed to writing the battles and victories of their confessions, we may entrust to everlasting memory those whom we believe to live forever and reign with Christ (cf. 2 Tim 2.12). But, most beloved brothers and sisters, I have difficulty with where to start or how to undertake the delightful confession of the most holy martyrs, i.e., with finding a beginning for my praise, because I am captivated by great events and by great virtues. Whatever I see in them, I admire it all as divine and heavenly: faith in their devotion, sanctity in their lives, constancy in their confessions, and victory in their sufferings. As much as these all shine forth like the sun in their [collective] virtues, so much are they all the more brilliant in the individual martyrs.

Now it seems good here at the beginning to treat the background of this war and to discuss the turning point which was decisive for the whole world. Of necessity, I must be brief and proceed with all speed so that, once the truth is recognized, one may know the rewards of the martyrs and the punishments of the traitors.[10]

§2   In the times of Diocletian and Maximian, the devil waged war against the Christians in this manner: he sought to burn the most holy testaments of the Lord, the divine scriptures, to destroy the basilicas of the Lord, and to prohibit the sacred rites and the most holy assemblies from celebrating in the Lord. But the army of the Lord did not accept such a monstrous order and it bristled at the sacrilegious command. Quickly it seized the arms of faith and descended into battle. This battle was to be fought not so much against human beings as against the devil (cf. Acts 5.29). Some fell from faith at the critical moment by handing over to unbelievers the scriptures of the Lord and the divine testaments so they could be burned in unholy fires. But how many more in preserving them bravely resisted by freely shedding their blood for them! When the devil had been completely defeated and ruined and all the martyrs were filled with God's

---

[10] All of §1 is lacking in Ruinart.

presence, bearing the palm[11] of victory over suffering, they sealed with their own blood the verdict against the traitors and their associates, rejecting them from the communion of the Church. For it was not right that there should be martyrs and traitors in the Church of God at the same time. Therefore, these enormous battle lines of confessors flew onto the field of combat from all sides, and where any of them found the enemy, there they pitched the camp of the Lord.

Now when the war trumpet sounded in the city of Abitina,[12] the glorious martyrs set up the standards of the Lord in the home of Octavius Felix.[13] While they were celebrating the sacraments of the Lord, as was their custom, they were taken into custody by the magistrates of the town[14] and by the soldier stationed there. Those arrested were Saturninus and his four children, i.e., Saturninus Jr. and Felix, the lectors; Maria, the consecrated virgin;[15] and the child Hilarianus. Also arrested were: Dativus, the one who was a senator, Felix, another Felix, Emeritus, Ampelius, Rogatianus, Quintus, Maximus, Telica, Rogatianus, Rogatus, Januarius, Cassianus, Victorianus, Vincentius, Cecelianus, Restituta, Prima, Eva, Rogatianus, Giualius, Rogatus, Pomponia, Secunda, Januaria, Saturnina, Martinus, Clautus, Felix, the elder Margarita, Honorata, Regiola, Victorinus, Pelusius, Faustus, Datianus, Matrona, Cecilia, Victoria, Hecretina, and another married woman named Januaria. These detainees were led briskly to the forum, now the first field of battle.

§3   Dativus went first, the one whom his holy parents bore, an upright senator in the heavenly senate house.[16] Then came the presbyter Saturninus surrounded by his numerous children. He chose some of them as his companions in martyrdom; he left the others to the Church as a memorial to his name. Following them came the army of the Lord. In it shone the splendor of heavenly armor: the shield of faith, the breastplate

---

[11] *Palma* is the token or symbol of victory and is translated iconographically into the palm branch borne by martyrs.

[12] Baluze has the name of the town sometimes as Alutina, other times as Aletina.

[13] Baluze: Occanus Felix.

[14] *Colonia*, a rural settlement.

[15] *Sanctimoniali*; see *The Passion of Maxima*, n. 24.

[16] As the army and civil administration have their ranks of honor, so too the Christians. Dativus holds the rank of *senator* in both the civil and, by analogy, the ecclesiastical spheres.

of justice, the helmet of salvation, and the sword[17] which is the word of God (Eph 6.14). Relying on this armor, they promised hope of victory to the brothers and sisters.

They came to the forum of the above-named city. Having been brought together there, they first bore the palm of confession to their arraignment before the magistrate. In this very same forum heaven had already battled on behalf of the scriptures of the Lord when Fundanus, formerly the bishop of the city, handed over the scriptures of the Lord to be burned. When the officials kindled the unholy fires under them, rain suddenly poured out of a clear sky. Just as the fire approached the holy scriptures, it was extinguished. Hail stones fell and the whole area was devastated by raging weather on behalf of the scriptures of the Lord.[18]

§4   Here the martyrs of Christ first received the chains they had longed for, and formed into a line, happy and cheerful, they sang hymns and songs to the Lord (cf. Eph 5.19) all along the road from this city to Carthage. When they arrived at the office of Anulinus who was then the proconsul, they stood in battle formation, steadfast and brave. Their steadfastness in the Lord beat back the blows of the raging devil. But when the fury of the devil could not prevail over all the soldiers of Christ together, he demanded them in combat one by one.

When it comes to the struggles of their battles I shall not proceed so much in my own words as in those of the martyrs so that the boldness of the raging enemy may be known in the torments and the sacrilegious invective, and the power of their leader Christ the Lord may be praised in the endurance of the martyrs and by their confession itself.

---

[17] The citation seems to lack *bifrons*, the *two-edged* sword. But B. N. Lat. 5297 does not have *bifrons* and the North African tradition often gives this verse without *bifrons*. See Tertullian, *Against Marcion* 3.14.4 (ANF 3.333); and Cyprian, *Ep.* 58.8 (ANF 5.350) and *Test.* 3.117 (ANF 5.556). Baluze (PL 8.691) and Ruinart (PL 8.705) have *bifrons* 'two-edged' to harmonize with the biblical verse.

[18] In *The Acts of Paul* §3.22 a similar downpour saves Thecla from martyrdom. See Hennecke, 2.361. *The Martyrdom of Saints Montanus and Lucius* §22 (Musurillo, p. 237) recounts a similar incident at Carthage. The motif of the elements in service of innocents is an ancient one, found as early as the story of Alkmena, the mother of Hercules. When her husband Amphitryon discovered her pregnancy by Zeus, he constructed a pyre on which to burn her. She called on Zeus to send rain to put out the fire, which he did.

§5   Therefore, since they were handed over by the local officials to
the proconsul and since it had been proposed that the Christians be sent
by the officials of Abitina—for they celebrated the Lord's Supper against
the prohibition of the emperors and the caesars—the proconsul first asked
Dativus what his station in life was and whether he had come to the
assembly. When he declared that he was a Christian and that he had come
to the assembly, the proconsul demanded the name of the leader of this
most holy assembly. Immediately he ordered the official on duty to put
Dativus on the rack and, once he was stretched out, to prepare the
claws.[19] The executioners carried out their cruel orders with dreadful
speed, and standing there filled with rage down to their fingertips,[20] with
the claws raised, they threatened the wounded sides of the martyr which
were already stripped and exposed.

Next Tazelita,[21] the bravest martyr, in front of everyone submitted
himself to torments and exclaimed, "We are Christians." He said, "We
do assemble." Then the anger of the proconsul blazed hot. Groaning and
severely wounded by a spiritual sword, the executioner struck the martyr
of Christ with heavy blows as he hung there on the rack. He stretched him
out and tore at him with the horrible grating claws. But in response, in
the midst of the fury of the executioners, Tazelita, the most glorious
martyr, poured out his prayer of thanksgiving to the Lord in this manner:
"Thanks be to God. In your name, O Christ, son of God, free your servants."

§6   In response to such a prayer the proconsul asked, "Who is the
leader of your congregation?" To the executioner now attacking more
fiercely he responded loudly, "Saturninus the presbyter and all of us."
O martyr, giving primacy to all! He does not give the presbyter priority
over the sisters and brothers but he joins them to the presbyter in the
fellowship of their confession. That is why he pointed to Saturninus when
the proconsul asked. He did not do it to single out the person whom he

---

[19] *Ungula*: an instrument of torture which scraped and gouged the sides of prisoners with
metal spikes like the talons of a bird.

[20] Most manuscripts have the difficult reading *indictis* which Franchi De'Cavalieri, p. 14,
amends to *indigitis*, making some sense of the otherwise incomprehensible reading in B.N.
17625 *indignitis*. For Franchi de'Cavalieri's version, see note 6 above.

[21] Baluze and Ruinart alone consistently have the name Thelica. See §2 for the name Telica.

saw fighting equally with him against the devil, but to explain fully that he celebrated in the assembly with them as their presbyter.[22]

Blood flowed out along with his voice as he prayed to the Lord, and, mindful of the precepts of the gospel, he asked for forgiveness for his enemies even as his body was being torn apart (cf. Matt 6.14 and Luke 23.34). Then in the midst of the most severe tortures of the blows he reproached his torturers and the proconsul equally with these words: "You act unjustly, you wretches, you struggle against God. O God most high, do not hold these sins against them (Acts 7.60). You are sinning, you wretches, you struggle against God. We keep[23] the precepts of God most high. You act unjustly, you wretches. You tear apart the innocent. We are not murderers. We are not criminals. O God, have mercy. To you be thanks. For your name's sake, give me endurance. Free your servants from the captivity of this world. To you be thanks. I cannot thank you enough."

His sides shook violently as claws bit into them like a plow. A wave of gore flowed out from the blood-red furrows. He heard the proconsul saying to him, "You are only beginning to feel what you ought to suffer." But Tazelita continued, "To glory. I thank you, God of all kingdoms. May the eternal kingdom come, an incorruptible kingdom. Lord Jesus, we are Christians; we serve you. You are our hope. You are the hope of Christians. God most holy, God most high, God omnipotent, we praise you for your name."

He prayed this way while the devil, through the judge, said, "You ought to obey the law of the emperors and the caesars." From a body now tormented, a victorious spirit answered with a strong and persistent voice, "I respect only the Law of God which I have learned. That is what I obey. I die for it. I am consumed by it, by the Law of God. There is no other (Deut 4.35)." By saying such things, it was the most glorious martyr himself who tormented Anulinus even worse than his own great tor-

---

[22] There seems to be some embarrassment for the narrator that Tazelita answered the question in such a way as to endanger the solidarity and equality of the confessors.

[23] Ruinart has *custodite* (the imperative) instead of *custodimus* (indicative), thereby diminishing the virtue of the Abitinians.

ments.[24] Finally, his anger fattened with ferocity, Anulinus said, "Stop," and he bound over to a well-deserved passion the martyr confined in his prison.

§7   Next Dativus was strengthened for battle by the Lord. He had been closely associated with Tazelita.[25] While he was tortured, he observed Tazelita hanging on the rack. Repeatedly Dativus bravely proclaimed that he was a Christian and had taken part in the assembly.

The brother of the most holy martyr Victoria[26] arrived on the scene. He was quite a distinguished Roman citizen, but at that time he was hostile to the practice of the most holy religion. Now he was reproving the martyr hung on the rack with unholy words, "Sir," he said, "this is the man who in the absence of our father kept trying to seduce our sister Victoria while we were studying here. He lured her from this most splendid city of Carthage all the way out to the town of Abitina along with Secunda and Restituta. He never came into our house except to lead their young hearts astray with his proselytizing."

But Victoria, the most distinguished martyr, did not endure her associate and fellow martyr being assailed by the lying senator. With Christian candor she immediately said, "No one persuaded me to leave and it was not with him that I went to Abitina. By the testimony of [free] citizens I can prove this: I did everything on my own initiative and by my own free will. Certainly I have been a member of the assembly; I have celebrated the Lord's Supper with my brothers and sisters because I am a Christian."

Then her shameless legal counsellor[27] flung even more foul-mouthed abuse against the martyr [Dativus]. But from his place on the rack, the glorious martyr refuted all the charges with his truthful rebuttal.

§8   Meanwhile Anulinus grew more angry and ordered the claws to be applied to the martyr. Immediately the executioners attacked his sides

---

[24] Anulinus' name is missing in Baluze. Note the reversal of the torturer and the victim, already seen in *The Passion of Maxima* §§2 and 5.

[25] Baluze adds: *ad fortissumum proelium* (for the bravest battle); Ruinart: *fortissimum proelium*.

[26] Some manuscripts insert his name Fortunatianus at this point. For the name, see §17.

[27] I.e., her brother, ironically the member of her family who would have been responsible for arranging for her defense.

which had been stripped and prepared for their blows by his bloody wounds. Their savage hands flew, more swift than their speedy orders. His skin was cut and his viscera torn. They laid open the recesses of his chest to the cruel gaze of the impious. In the midst of these events, the mind of the martyr stands firm and even if his limbs were broken, his viscera torn to pieces and his sides ripped apart, nevertheless, the soul of the martyr endures whole and unshaken. Finally, mindful of his dignity (2 Macc 6.23), Dativus the senator poured out his prayer to the Lord as follows in the presence of the mad executioner: "O Christ, Lord, let me not be put to shame (Ps 30.18)." With these words the most blessed martyr merited so easily what he had so succinctly requested from the Lord.

Finally now, the mind of the proconsul was deeply disturbed. In spite of himself[28] he burst forth: "Stop!" The executioners stopped, for it was not right that the martyr of Christ should be tortured for the sake of Victoria his co-martyr.

§9   Although Pompeianus the savage prosecutor attacked him with unjustified suspicion and initiated a slanderous suit [against him], the martyr fixed a look on him and deeply affected him saying: "What are you doing in this place, you devil? What are you trying to do to the martyrs of Christ?" The senator of the Lord and martyr overcame both the power and rage of this lawyer. But how the most famous martyr had to be racked for Christ! Questioned whether he had been in the assembly, he firmly confessed and said that when there was an assembly, he had come; along with his sisters and brothers he had celebrated the Lord's supper with a devotion befitting his religion; and that there was[29] one single organizer of this most holy assembly. This again so readily incited the proconsul against him and his savagery broke out again. The dignity of the martyr is redoubled as he is flogged with the furrowing claws. But the martyr tormented in the midst of his most cruel wounds repeated his original prayer: "I beseech you, O Christ, let me not be put to shame (Ps 30.18). What have I done? Saturninus is our presbyter."

§10   While the harsh and grim executioners scraped Dativus' sides with

---

[28] *Nolente* is missing in Ruinart; *volente* (willingly) is found in Baluze.

[29] Ruinart adds: *non*, not. See n. 22.

crooked claws, as if their teacher were Cruelty itself showing them the way, Saturninus the presbyter is summoned to the battle. In his contemplation of the heavenly kingdom, he considers these things truly small and of no consequence. He began to support his fellow martyrs and to fight alongside them. The proconsul said, "You acted against the order of the emperors and the caesars when you gathered all of these people together." Saturninus the presbyter, with the prompting of the Spirit of the Lord, fearlessly responded, "We celebrated the Lord's supper."

The proconsul said, "Why?" He responded, "Because it was not possible to neglect the Lord's supper." When Saturninus had said these things, the proconsul immediately ordered Dativus to be prepared for torture. Dativus meanwhile watched the tearing of his body rather than grieve. His mind and spirit depended on the Lord. He thought nothing of the pain in his body but only prayed to the Lord saying, "Come to my aid, I pray. O Christ, have pity on my soul. Care for my spirit. Let me not be put to shame, I pray, O Christ."

The proconsul said to him, " It would have been better if you had called others from this most splendid city to a right disposition and if you had not acted against the order of the emperors and the caesars." But steadfastly and constantly he cried out, "I am a Christian." Overcome by this reply, this devil said, "Stop!" Throwing him also into prison, the proconsul set this martyr aside for a worthy passion.

§11   But while the presbyter Saturninus hung on the rack anointed by the newly shed blood of the martyrs, he was incited to persist in the faith of those in whose blood he stood fast. While he was being interrogated whether he had been the organizer and whether he had gathered everyone together, he said, "I was there in the assembly." Contending alongside the presbyter, Emeritus the lector springing up for battle said, "I am the organizer in whose home the assemblies were held." But by now the proconsul had so often been gotten the better of that he shook with horror at the attack of Emeritus. Nevertheless, turning toward the presbyter, he said, "Why did you act against the order? What do you get out of confessing?"[30] Saturninus said to him, "The Lord's supper could not be neglect-

---

[30] This sentence is missing in Ruinart and Baluze.

ed; so the Law orders."[31] Then the proconsul said, "Nonetheless, you should not have made light of what was forbidden but rather you should have observed the order of the emperors and not acted against them." And with a voice well practiced against the martyrs, he admonished the torturers to begin to torment him.[32]

He is obeyed with willing compliance. The executioners fall on the elderly body of the presbyter and, with their anger raging, they tear the broken bonds of his sinews. You should have seen the lamentable tortures and the exquisite torments of a new kind inflicted on the priest of God. You should have seen the executioners vent their anger as if they had a rabid hunger for wounds as food and for the entrails now open to the horror of those watching. Amidst the red of the blood, the bones gleamed white. Lest his soul being pressed out from his body desert it in the delays between rackings, the presbyter prayed to the Lord in this way: "I beseech you, O Christ, hear me. I give you thanks, O God. Order me to be beheaded. I beseech you, O Christ, have mercy. Son of God, come to my aid."

The proconsul said to him, "Why do you act against the order?"

The presbyter said, "Thus does the Law order. Thus does the Law teach." O divine reply of the learned presbyter, truly wondrous enough to be proclaimed! Even under torture the presbyter preaches the most holy Law for which he freely withstood torture. At last, frightened by the mention of the Law, Anulinus said, "Stop!" Throwing him back into the confinement of prison he destined him for the suffering for which he hoped.

§12   Once Emeritus was charged, the proconsul said, "Were assemblies held in your home against the order of the emperor?" Emeritus filled with the Holy Spirit said to him, "We did hold the Lord's supper in my home." In reply the proconsul said, "Why did you permit them to enter?" He responded, "Because they are my brothers and sisters and I could not prevent them from doing so." Then the proconsul said, "You should have prevented them." In response Emeritus said, "I could not because we

---

[31] North Africans, especially Donatists, often refer to the Bible as the Law.

[32] Thus Ruinart: *tortorem saevire commonuit*; other readings offer: *terrorem suae irae commonuit* (He brought to mind the horror of his anger).

cannot go without the Lord's supper."

At once the proconsul ordered him to be stretched out on the rack, and once stretched out, to be tortured. After new executioners came on duty, while he was suffering heavy blows, he said, "I beseech you, O Christ, come to my aid. You wretches are the ones acting against the command of God (cf. Acts 5.29)."

The proconsul interrupted, "You should not have admitted them." Emeritus responded, "I could not but admit my brothers and sisters." Then the sacrilegious proconsul said, "But the order of the emperors and the caesars takes priority." In reply the most pious martyr said, "God is greater—and not the emperors.[33] I pray, O Christ. Praise to you. Give me endurance."

The proconsul interrupted him as he prayed, "Do you have any scriptures in your home?" He responded, "I have them but they are in my heart (2 Cor 3.3)." "Do you have them in your home, he said, "or do you not?" Emeritus the martyr said, "I have them in my heart. I plead, Christ. Praise to you. Free me, Christ. I suffer in your name.[34] Briefly do I suffer; freely do I suffer, O Christ (cf. 2 Macc 6.30). Lord, let me not be put to shame (Ps 30.18)."

O martyr, mindful of the Apostle who had the Law of the Lord written "not in stone but by the Spirit of the living God, not on tablets of stone but in the tablets of the fleshy heart (2 Cor 3.3)"! O martyr, most suitable and diligent custodian of the sacred Law! Trembling at the crime of the traitors, he placed the scriptures of the Lord within the recesses of his own heart lest he lose them. Once he heard this, the proconsul said, "Stop!" and recalling to memory Emeritus' profession,[35] along with the rest of the confessions, he said, "For all your misdeeds, you will pay the punishment merited by your confession."

§13   But now with his countenance changed, the proconsul's wild rage faded, appeased by the torments of the martyrs. But when Felix, both by

---

[33] Baluze: *Deus, inquit, major est quam imperatores* ("God," he said, "is greater than the emperors").

[34] Baluze omits *patior*, I suffer.

[35] Here and elsewhere Baluze consistently has *confessio* for *professio*. In early Christian literature the former is almost universally positive, a statement of true faith. *Professio*, however, is often used for the statement of (erroneous) faith by a heretic.

name and in his suffering,[36] had marched forward into combat and the
entire battle line of the Lord stood uninjured and unconquered, the tyrant's
mind was destroyed, his voice dispirited, his soul and body torn asun-
der.[37] He said, "I hope that you will choose to obey orders so that you
may live." In response the confessors of the Lord, the unconquered
martyrs of Christ, spoke as if with one voice: "We are Christians. We
can do no other than to keep the Law of the Lord even unto the shedding
of blood." Battered by such speech, the enemy said to Felix, "I am not
asking whether you are Christians but whether you held assemblies or
whether you have any scriptures." O stupid and laughable inquiry of the
judge! He said, "If you are a Christian, shut up about it," and he added,
"Answer[38] whether you were in the assembly." As if one could be a
Christian without the Lord's Supper or the Lord's Supper could be
celebrated without a Christian! Or do you not know, O Satan, that the
Christian exists through the Lord's Supper and the Lord's Supper in Christians? Neither can exist without the other. When you hear the Name, learn
about the gathering of the Lord, and when you hear 'assemblies' recognize
the Name. Then it is you who will be examined by the martyr and it is
you who will be mocked; with such a reply you will be confounded. Felix
added, "We celebrated the most glorious assembly. We always gathered
to read the scriptures of the Lord at the Lord's Supper."

Deeply disturbed by this profession,[39] Anulinus united to the heavenly
council the lifeless martyr who had been struck down by the blows of
cudgels and was at that moment hastening to the heavenly judgment seat
now that his suffering has been completed.

§14   But another Felix follows Felix, equal in name and confession,
similar in his very suffering. Contending with equal strength, he was
battered by blows of cudgels. Laying down his life in the torments of
prison, he was united with the previous Felix as a martyr.

After these, Ampelius, guardian of the Law and most faithful protector

---

[36] His name means 'happy' or 'fortunate'.
[37] Compare the effects of the torture of the martyrs on the body of the man who ordered
the torture with the similar effects in *The Passion of Maxima* §5, n. 39.
[38] Baluze has *respondit* (he answered) for *responde*.
[39] Again Baluze has *confessio* for *professio*.

of divine scripture, took up the contest. When the proconsul asked whether he was part of the assembly, lighthearted and secure he answered with a vigorous voice. He said, "I held an assembly with my brothers and sisters, I celebrated the Lord's supper, and I have with me the scriptures of the Lord. They are written in my heart (2 Cor 3.3). Christ, I give you praise. Hear me, Christ." When he had said these things, he was bruised about the neck. He was happy to be bound up with his brothers, there in prison, like a light[40] in the tabernacle of the Lord (cf. Exod 25.31ff).

Rogatianus followed him. Having confessed the name of the Lord, he was joined unharmed to the aforementioned brothers.

Then Quintus, having been charged and having confessed the name of the Lord uncommonly well, magnificently, was struck down by blows and thrust into jail, to be held for a well-deserved martyrdom.

Maximus followed him, his counterpart in confession, similar in combat, equal in the triumph of victory.

Following him, the younger Felix proclaimed the Lord's supper as the hope and salvation of Christians. He himself fell, similarly beset by blows. He said, "With a faithful spirit, I celebrated the Lord's supper. I held an assembly with my brothers and sisters because I am a Christian." By this confession, he became worthy to be associated with his aforementioned brothers.

§15 Now the younger Saturninus, the holy[41] offspring of the priest Saturninus, quickly approached the anticipated battle, hastening to equal the most glorious virtues of his father. The proconsul under the influence of the devil said to him, "And you, Saturninus, were you mixed up in this?"

Saturninus responded, "I am a Christian." The proconsul said, "I didn't ask you that, but whether you attended the Lord's supper."

Saturninus responded, "I attended the Lord's supper because Christ is the saviour." When he heard the name of the saviour, Anulinus grew angry and prepared the rack used on the father for the son. When Saturninus had been stretched out, he said, "Saturninus, what evidence do you offer? Consider your situation. Do you have any scriptures?" Saturninus

---

[40] Baluze and Ruinart has *iam* (now) instead of *lumen* (light).
[41] Baluze omits *sancta* (holy) before *progenies* (offspring).

responded, "I am a Christian."

The proconsul said: "I am asking whether you assembled and whether you have any scriptures." He responded, "I am a Christian. There is no one else[42] we ought to consider holy except Christ (cf. Acts 4.12)."

The devil, enraged by this confession, said, "Because you have remained obstinate, it is fitting to question you by torture to see whether you have any scriptures." And he said to the officials, "Torture him."

The weary torturers attacked the sides of the son[43] with lacerations like those of his father and they mixed the father's blood which had moistened the claws with the corresponding blood of the son. Through the furrows of the open wounds you saw the father's blood dripping from the sides of the son and the blood of the son mixed with the father's dripping from the moistened claws. But the youth, reinvigorated by the mixture of familial blood, felt it a healing remedy rather than torment. Fortified by his torments, he exclaimed with loud cries, "I have the scriptures of the Lord, but I have them in my heart (2 Cor 3.3). I beg you, Christ, give me endurance. In you there is hope (Eccl 24.25)."[44]

Anulinus said, "Why did you act against the order?"

He responded, "Because I am a Christian."

When he heard that, Anulinus said, "Stop," and as soon as the torments were discontinued, Saturninus was joined in fellowship with his father.

§16   Meanwhile day slid into night as the hours slipped away, and, with torments swallowed up like the sun, the madness of the exhausted torturers grew faint[45] along with the cruelty of the judge. But the legions of the Lord, in whom Christ the eternal light shone forth with the flashing brightness of heavenly armor,[46] bravely and constantly sprang forth into combat.

The adversary of the Lord was conquered by the most glorious striving of so many martyrs and was overcome by so many and so great a crowd. Deserted by day, attacked by night, abandoned now that the anger of the

---

[42] Ruinart adds *nomen*, 'no other *name*', to conform to the biblical verse.

[43] Baluze has *antea* (before) for *nati* (of the son).

[44] Baluze has *Spes est vitae* (he [Christ] is the hope for life).

[45] Baluze: *profligaturus* (future) for *profligatus* (perfect).

[46] Ruinart has *annorum* (years) for *armorum*.

executioners was dissipating, he was not able to fight with them one by one, so he strictly interrogates the souls of the whole army of the Lord and he strikes at the devoted minds of the confessors[47] with this sort of interrogation: "You have seen,"[48] he said, "what those who have persevered have sustained and what they still have to sustain if they stand firm in their confession. Therefore, let any one of you who wishes to acquire a pardon make a deposition in order to be saved."

In reply, the confessors of the Lord, the glorious martyrs of Christ, simultaneously joyful and triumphant (not on account of the proconsul's word but on account of victory in suffering), burning with the Holy Spirit, said strongly and clearly, as if with one voice, "We are Christians." By this utterance, the devil was laid low and Anulinus was struck down. Deeply disturbed and throwing them all into jail, he bound over the holy ones for martyrdom.

§17   And lest the most devoted sex of women and the brightest band of holy virgins be deprived of the glory of such a battle, all of the women, with the help of Christ the Lord, were brought in and crowned in victory. Now Victoria, the holiest of the women, the flower of virgins, the glory and grandeur of confessors, came from a respectable family. She was most devoted to her religion and temperate in her morals. In her the goodness of nature shone forth in brilliant modesty. To the beauty of her body there corresponded in her mind an even more beautiful faith and integrity of holiness. She rejoiced in the second pledge of victory granted to her in martyrdom for the Lord.[49]

Clear signs of her virtue had been shining forth from her very infancy. Even in her tender years, a most chaste firmness of mind and a sure worthiness for her future suffering appeared. Finally, after total virginity complemented the mature[50] part of her life, and when the young woman unwillingly and reluctantly was forced into a marriage and her parents gave her a bridegroom against her will, the young woman secretly threw herself off a cliff so that she might flee the man who would carry her off

---

[47] Baluze and Ruinart has *sanctorum* (saints) for *confessorum* (confessors).

[48] *Vidistis* (you have seen) is not in Ruinart.

[49] The first pledge had been her arrest at Abitina.

[50] For *adultum*, Baluze has *ultimum* (final).

like booty.[51] Supported by compliant breezes, she was received unharmed on the lap of the earth.[52] She should not have had to suffer for Christ since she had already died for the sake of her singular modesty.

Therefore, freed from marriage and at the same time from both an abusive bridegroom and her parents, leaping forth almost from the very midst of the crowd at the wedding, the unconquered virgin took refuge at the house of modesty and the harbor of chastity, the Church. There with unblemished honor she reserved the most holy hair of her head, consecrated and dedicated to God in perpetual virginity.[53] Then, hurrying on to martyrdom, she held before her in her right hand the flowering palm of triumphant modesty.

When the proconsul asked her what she professed, she responded with a clear voice, "I am a Christian." When Fortunatianus, her distinguished brother and counselor, said that her mind had been captivated by inane arguments, Victoria responded: "My mind is made up," she said, "I've never changed."

In response the proconsul said, "Do you want to go with Fortunatianus your brother?"

She answered, "I do not want to because I am a Christian and my brothers are those who keep the commands of God."[54] O young woman, strengthened by the authority of divine Law! O glorious virgin rightly consecrated to the eternal king! O most blessed martyr, most famous for her evangelical profession! With a dominical saying she responded: "My

---

[51] Baluze: "when the young woman unwillingly and reluctantly was forced into marriage by her parents and she suggested that she be unwillingly handed over to a husband as booty, the young woman secretly threw herself off a cliff."

[52] See *The Passion of Maxima* §4 for another young woman's defenestration in the face of a forced marriage, and *The Martyrdom of Marculus* §13 for martyrdom by precipitation. In this latter case, the earth cares for the body of the saint. On the Christian reconstruction of suicide as a dishonorable alternative to the loss of virginity, see Dennis Trout, "Re-textualizing Lucretia: Cultural Subversion in the *City of God*," *Journal of Early Christian Studies* 2/1 (1994), pp. 53-70.

[53] Among North African Christians hairstyle indicated a woman's marital status. See Cyprian, *On the Dress of Virgins* §5 (ANF 5.430) and Optatus §6.4 (Vassall-Phillips, p. 259).

[54] In this context, the biblical referent would be less likely Mt 12.46-50 than the many times keeping the commandments is referred to in Deuteronomy and Revelation. Cf. 2 Macc. 7.37.

brothers are those who keep the commands of God."

When he heard these words, Anulinus, laying aside the authority of his office, stepped down to reason with the young woman. "Have some regard for your situation," he said. "You see that your brother is concerned with providing for your welfare." The martyr of Christ said to him, "My mind is made up. I've never changed. I was in the assembly and I celebrated the Lord's supper with the sisters and brothers because I am a Christian."

As soon as he heard these things, Anulinus raging, agitated, and burning with anger, chained the most holy young woman, the martyr of Christ, in prison, along with the others. He reserved them all for suffering like the Lord's.[55]

§18   But Hilarianus, one of the children of the presbyter-martyr Saturninus, still remained. He overcame his diminutive age with his great devotion. Rushing to be united to the triumph of his father and brothers, he scarcely feared the dire threats of the tyrant because he reckoned them as nothing. When it was said to him, "Are you imitating your father or your brothers?" suddenly a youthful voice is heard from his tiny body and the little heart of the boy is opened to a full confession of the Lord in his response: "I am a Christian, and of my own will and volition I attended the assembly with my father and brothers."

Have you not been listening to the voice of his father Saturninus the martyr coming from the sweet lips of his son! Have you not been listening to the tongue confessing Christ as Lord, secure in the example of his brother! But the stupid proconsul did not realize that he was not fighting against humans beings but against God (Acts 5.29) because he did not notice the great spirit in his youthful years. He thought the boy could be terrified with infantile torments. At last he said, "I'll cut off your hair and nose and ears and I'll release[56] you that way (cf. 2 Macc 7.3)."

The child Hilarianus, glorious in the virtues of his father and brothers, had already learned from his elders to disdain torments; to these remarks he responded with a clear voice: "Do whatever you wish to do, for I am a Christian." Soon he too is ordered to be taken back into the prison and

---

[55] Baluze: "like the Lord's" is missing, denying the Donatists' martyrs any likeness to the Lord of the Catholics.

[56] Baluze and Ruinart have *dimitto* (present tense) for *dimittam* (future tense).

the voice of Hilarianus is heard saying with great joy: "Thanks be to God."

Here one battle in the great war is brought to an end; here the devil is overcome and conquered; here the martyrs of Christ rejoice with eternal joy concerning the eternal glory of their future suffering.[57]

§19[58] For truly, as we have already said, the time of schism admonishes us by so many and such great confessions to collect the pronouncements of the martyrs and to link the most holy injunctions of the friends of God to the preceding deeds. By necessity I shall review only briefly all those things which the martyrs in prison did ordain on the basis of divine Law and which they leave reserved for those who succeed them. In my haste I shall omit neither the arrogance of the lapsed nor the impudence of the traitors because faith, love of the Law, the condition of the Church, public welfare and the common life force me to omit nothing that happened. Based on this account, one will be able to recognize which church is the Catholic Church, if the pestiferous defect of the traitors is revealed for all ages by their impious deeds as well as by the judgment of the martyrs.

Therefore, after the long-desired prison received the above mentioned martyrs of Christ, the confessors there, whose cases had already been postponed, joined their triumphant right hands to the hands of the victors as they entered. Moreover, many other confessors came to that same place from diverse parts of the province. Among them were bishops, presbyters, deacons and others of clerical rank. They all upheld the Law of the Lord and steadfastly and bravely celebrated the assembly of the Lord. They saved the scriptures of the Lord and the divine testaments from flames and burning. For the sake of the divine Law, they offered their very selves to menacing fires and diverse tortures in the manner of the Maccabees (cf. 2 Macc 6.1-7.42).

§20   Even though in this calamity the terrible prison and thick darkness held the most faithful witnesses of God closed up within them and subdued their faithful members with the heavy weight of chains, even though hunger weakened them, thirst exhausted them, and cold battered them,

---

[57] The narrative does not include their executions which take place, according to the introduction, at various times and places.

[58] §§19-23 are not found in Ruinart.

and the crowd pressed the very sides broken at last by a recent mangling with claws, nevertheless, gathering together as a council, amidst chains of iron and all the instruments of torture, on the authority of divine Law, they established a heavenly decree which the martyrs preserved for themselves and their descendants.

Truly the living Spirit, the Holy Spirit, directed the minds of the confessors by infusing them with eternal and divine discourse. Then after the cruel calamity and the horrible threats of persecution, when by these threats tyrannical rage had attacked the Christian religion, so that the eternal peace of the Christian Name might shine ever more pure and more serene, there was lacking neither intense deception on the part of all those traitors nor the conspiracy of the noxious remainder of those whose faith had been shipwrecked. These were brought together by diabolical art which, under the guise of religion, attacked faith, overturned law and disturbed divine authority. When Mensurius, so-called bishop of Carthage, polluted by the recent handing over of scripture, repented of the malice of his misdeeds and then began to reveal greater crimes, he who had had to beg and implore from the martyrs' pardon for burning the books, raged against the martyrs with the same resolve with which he had handed over the divine laws, thus adding to his transgressions even more shameful acts. More ruthless than the tyrant, more bloody than the executioner, he chose Caecilian his deacon as a suitable minister of his misdeeds and he stationed him before the doors of the prison, armed with whips and lashes so he might turn away from the entrance and exit all those who brought food and drink to the martyrs in prison, further harming those already wronged by grave injustice. People who came to nourish the martyrs were struck down right and left by Caecilian. The cups for the thirsty inside in chains were broken. At the entrance to the prison food was scattered only to be torn apart by the dogs. Before the doors of the prison the fathers of the martyrs fell and the most holy mothers. Shut out from the sight of their children,[59] they kept their vigil day and night at the entrance of the prison. There was the dreadful weeping and the bitter lamentation by all who were there. To keep the pious from the embrace of the martyrs and to keep Christians from a duty of piety, Caecilian was more ruthless than

---

[59] Baluze has *excussi* (forced out or away) rather than *exclusi* (shut out).

the tyrant, more bloody than the executioner.

§21   Meanwhile neither the squalor of prison nor the pain of the flesh nor, finally, the lack of anything disturbed the martyrs of Christ. But already near to the Lord by their merits and their confession, they directed those who succeeded them, the renewed progeny of the Christian name, to be separated from all filth and communion with traitors by this warning: "If anyone communicates with the traitors, that person will have no part with us in the heavenly kingdom." And they endorsed this verdict of theirs by the authority of the Holy Spirit written in such evidence: "It is written," they said, "in the Apocalypse, 'Whoever adds to this book one part of a letter or one letter, to him will the Lord add innumerable afflictions. And whoever blots them out, so will the Lord blot out his share from the Book of Life (Rev 22.18-19).' If, therefore, a part of a letter added or a letter omitted cuts off a person at the roots from the Book of Life (cf. 2 Macc 7.9) and if such constitutes a sacrilege, it is necessary that all those who handed over the divine testaments and the honored laws of the omnipotent God and of the Lord Jesus Christ to be burned in profane fires should be tormented in the eternal flames of Gehenna and inextinguishable fire. And, therefore, as we have already said, 'If anyone communicates with the traitors, that person will not have a share with us in the heavenly kingdom.'"

Sharing in these judgments, one by one, they hurried off to the glory of suffering and to the ultimate testimony. Each one of the martyrs signed the judgment with their own blood. Accordingly, the Holy Church follows the martyrs and curses the treachery of the traitor Mensurius.[60]

§22   Therefore, these things being so, would anyone who is strong in the knowledge of divine law, endowed with faith, outstanding in devotion and most holy[61] in religion, who realizes that God the Judge discerns truth from error, distinguishes faith from faithlessness, and isolates false pretense from sure and intact holiness, God who separates the upright from the lapsed, the unimpaired from the wounded, the just

---

[60] Baluze and some manuscripts do not include the name of Mensurius; these appear to have been edited to blame the crime on the traitors as a group without mentioning the Catholic bishop by name.

[61] Baluze: *sanctus* (holy); all others have *sanctissimus* (most holy).

from the guilty, the innocent from the condemned, the custodian of the Law from the traitor, the confessor of the name of Christ from the denier, the martyr of the Lord from the persecutor, would that person think that the church of the martyrs and the conventicle of traitors is one and the same thing? Of course, no one does. For these repel each other so and they are as contrary to each other as light is to darkness, life to death, a holy angel to the devil, Christ to the Antichrist. As Paul the Apostle said: "Open your hearts to me as children and do not be joined to unbelievers. For what sharing is there between justice and iniquity or what communion between light and darkness? What accord is there between Christ and Belial,[62] what small share between a believer and an unbeliever, what agreement between the temple of God and idols? For you are the temple of the living God. He says, 'I will live in them and I will walk among them and I will be their God and they shall be my people. Because of this, go out from their midst and separate,' says the Lord God almighty, 'and do not touch the unclean and I will take you back and I will be a father to you and you shall be my sons and daughters,' says the Lord almighty (2 Cor 6.13-18)."

On account of this, the good must flee the conspiracy of the traitors, the home of hypocrites, and the judgments of the Pharisees, and the devout must always avoid them. Would that those spiritually born should worthily succeed to adoption as the sons and daughters of God in the holy Church and would that they not be sunk in the crimes of others, acquiring darkness instead of light, death instead of life, destruction instead of salvation! Such is the nature of the Church of the Lord that I do not say "this part" because it is one alone and cannot be split or divided into two parts. But after the horrible night of persecution and the pestilential whirlwinds of tyrants, the Devil by a craftiness of the most adroit fraud devises for himself a council of the shipwrecked[63] to deceive the innocent and to plunder the people. Thus if he cannot swallow down people in the clear disaster of persecution and he cannot hold them fast in the bonds of transgression in a sacrilegious sect in the service of idols for their everlasting destruction, joining those to himself with polluted traitors, he destroys

---

[62] Baluze alone omits this clause.

[63] I. e., of those who have denied their faith. Cf. Cyprian, *On the Lapsed* 15 (ANF 5.441).

them under the pretext of most holy religion. Then spurious rites of the holy and pretended mysteries[64] are celebrated not so much for salvation as for the ruin of those wretches, since the impious man erects the altar, the profane celebrates the sacraments, the guilty baptizes, the wounded cures, the persecutor venerates the martyrs, the traitor reads the Gospel, the one who burned the divine testaments promises the inheritance of heaven. It is these whom the Lord rebukes and reproves in the gospel saying: "Woe to you, Scribes and Pharisees, hypocrites, for you circle the sea and the dry land to make a single proselyte. And when you have made him, you make him a son of Gehenna more duplicitous than you yourselves are (Mt 23.15)." Rejecting their polluted sacrifices, he said through the prophet: "Their sacrifices are like the bread of affliction; anyone who has touched it will be defiled (Hos 9.4)." Through Haggai the most famous prophet: "The Lord says 'Ask the priests about the law. If a person receives consecrated meat in the fold of the garment and the fold of the garment touches another portion of bread, wine, or oil, will it be made holy? And the priests will say, "No."' And the Lord said, 'If a person polluted in his soul touched anything of these things, will it be polluted?' And the priests said, "It will be polluted."' The Lord said, 'Thus it is with this people and this nation before me.' So says the Lord and whoever will be like this will be polluted (Hag 2.12-13)."

§23   Therefore, one must flee and curse the whole corrupt congregation of all the polluted people and all must seek the glorious lineage of the blessed martyrs, which is the one, holy, and true Church, from which the martyrs arise and whose divine mysteries[65] the martyrs observe. She and she alone broke the force of infernal persecution; she preserved the law of the Lord even to the shedding of blood. In her the virtues of the people are cultivated in the presence of the Holy Spirit, saving baptism is performed, life is renewed forever. God remains ever merciful to them. The Lord Christ is here and with the Holy Spirit rejoices and is glad, victor among the confessors, conqueror among the martyrs.

[At last, since neither Mensurius nor his minister Caecilian wished to pull back from this monstrous cruelty, and Anulinus the proconsul and

---

[64] *Mysteria* (mysteries) is a technical term for the sacraments.

[65] Baluze alone has *testamenta* (scriptures) rather than *mysteria*.

the other persecutors were occupied meanwhile with other business, these blessed martyrs, deprived of bodily nourishment, little by little over a period of days, forced by the atrocity of hunger, left their natural state and migrated to the heavenly realms with their palm of martyrdom, led by our Lord Jesus Christ who with the Father reigns forever and ever. Amen.[66]]

This is the end of the confessions and the judicial record of the martyrs Saturninus the presbyter and his companions.[67]

---

[66] This paragraph occurs in none of the surviving manuscripts but only in one of the sources for the edition of Baluze which was published in Migne. It appears to be an attempt to account for the deaths of the martyrs, not otherwise narrated. As such, it hardly accords with the opening paragraph of the story which has them meeting their deaths at various times in different places.

[67] This paragraph is not recorded in Baluze.

A Sermon on the Passion of Saints Donatus and Advocatus Given on the 4th Day before the Ides of March

Introduction

In 311 Donatists refused to accept the ordination of Caecilian as bishop of Carthage. They ordained their own bishop, Majorinus, and appealed to the emperor Constantine for recognition as the true Church in North Africa. Constantine impanelled a commission of bishops at Rome in 312 to judge between the parties supporting Caecilian and Majorinus. The commission vindicated Caecilian. The dissidents refused to accept the judgment and appealed again to the emperor. In response, Constantine formed a second episcopal commission, this time composed of bishops from Gaul. When their judgment in favor of Caecilian was not accepted, Constantine commissioned a military force to pacify the dissidents.

This sermon dates from the first period of the repression of the Donatists (317-321) when membership in the pro- and anti-Caecilianist groups was still fluid. Inspirational sermons or the offer of governmental subsidies might sway individuals or entire congregations to change allegiance.

Contrary to its traditional title, it does not contain accounts of saints named Donatus and Advocatus. The title may come from a combination of two facts. First, the sermon is attributed to Donatus, the eponymous founder of the movement. Second, the sermon records, *inter alia*, the martyrdom of the unnamed bishop of the town of Avioccala. The name of the town may have been transmuted to the personal name Advocatus.

Stories of a mass martyrdom and of the torture and execution of the bishop are set within a sermon designed at its climax to inflame cate-chumens with a desire to follow their fellow citizens and the revered bishop into glory. The sermon is thought to have been delivered not long after the events narrated, between 317 and 320.[1] Like *The Acts of the Abitinian Martyrs*, it survives in versions which are labelled 'Donatist' and 'Catholic'. The Donatist version again is the earlier of the two and is the one used here.[2] The text is from PL 8.752-58. A lightly edited version is printed in Maier 1.201-211.

TRANSLATION

§1   If we have not written in vain of well-known acts of persecution, and on this annual solemnity we read them not unadvisedly in honor of the martyrs and for the edification of believers, why don't we likewise write and read of cunning deceits and seductive snares of deception, those deeds which by dishonest fraud destroy souls under the pretext of religion. Instruction is even more necessary when there is no obvious contention on an issue, because it is easy for a belligerent group to mislead someone, especially when it is one's nearest neighbor. "And one's foes," the Bible says, "will be members of one's own household" (Mt 10.36 and Mi 7.6).

Now then, suppressing the praises of the martyrs out of envious silence is contrary to the obligations of religion and piety. So also is hiding what is beneficial under the protection of misleading silence. It is as dangerous for the prudent not to speak of this as it is injurious to the honest not to understand. As it is indeed easy for the unwary to be deceived by liars

---

[1] Jean-Paul Brisson, *Autonomisme et Christianisme dans l'Afrique romaine de Septime Sévère à l'invasion vandale* (Paris: Boccard, 1958), p. 310, considers it a sermon of Donatus preached in March 318 or 319. Frend, *TDC*, p. 321 (cf. pp. 159-60), makes no claims about the identity of the author, but ascribes it to the year 320. For a summary of various arguments concerning the dating of the text see "Der *Sermo de passione sanctorum Donati et Advocati* als donatistisches Selbstzeugnis" by Knut Schäferdiek in *Oecumenica et Patristica: Festschrift für Wilhelm Schneemelcher zum 75. Geburstag*, edited by Damaskinos Papandreou, Wolfgang A. Bienert and Knut Schäferdiek (Stuttgart, Berlin and Cologne: W. Kohlhammer, 1989), pp. 175-98, specifically, pp. 176-77.

[2] François Dolbeau, "La Passion des saints Lucius et Montanus: Histoire et édition du texte," *REA* 29 (1983), pp. 64-65.

who use the name of Christ, so also it is necessary for the ministers of the Antichrist to flee from that Name. Therefore, when one discovers wolves hiding in sheep's clothing, either those who were deceived by ignorance will be set free (once they are instructed) or the insolent will perish in their vice (without Christian preaching being at fault or in any danger). Thus, there is a reason for exposing what has been done, and it is fully beneficial and just, because the faithful are being strengthened by recalling these events and the neophytes whom they stir up to bear their trials are also strengthened, and by discovering their enemies, they learn to condemn them.

Therefore, may sweet mother Church proclaim the enduring faith of her children. May the den of the most cruel thieves call to mind the fruit of their work (cf. Mt 21.13).

§2   Now then, let's proceed with the situation. The incident occurred at Carthage when Caecilian Eudinepisus[3] was there, and Leontius had been appointed *comes*, Ursatius was *dux*, Marcellinus tribune, and the Devil appeared as counsellor for all of them.[4] Their practices were rooted in the old Serpent[5] who had already showed himself the enemy of the Christian Name. By deceitful fraud, he strove to lay hold of those he could not conquer by direct persecution. The author of deception lay hidden so that his deception might proceed more easily. But divine precepts are always the arms of victory for those who recognize the snares of the Flatter, and they are not frightened by his raging harassment.

So the hostile contriver did not deceive the wary and vigilant by his

---

[3] This appellation appears to be not a surname but a misreading of *pseudoepiscopus*, the so-called (and thus false) bishop.

[4] Caecilian was the Catholic bishop. Little is known of the others, all Roman officials. Leontius was *comes* in Africa 317-321. Ursatius is known from Augustine's works as a prime persecutor of Donatists. See *Contra litteras Petiliani* 2.92.202 and *Contra Cresconium* 3.30.34 (CSEL 52.125 and 441). Marcellinus was tribune in Africa 317-321 and is not to be confused with the friend of Augustine by the same name who convoked the Conference of Carthage in 411. As tribune, he commanded a military unit on the frontier. For a discussion of these offices, see above, "Legal and Literary Notes," n. 40, the articles *comites*, *dux*, and *tribunus* by Henry M. D. Parker in *The Oxford Classical Dictionary*, 2nd ed., edited by N. G. L. Hammond and H. H. Scullard (Oxford: Clarendon, 1970), and those by Otto Seeck in *PW*.

[5] I.e., Satan.

charming conduct. The people whom he long ago publicly humiliated could have been brought back by penance to Him whom they had denied. The Lord himself does not wish the death of the one who is perishing but rather that that person should return and live (cf. Ezek 33.11). He was ready to receive the confession of those who were sorry. Knowing this, when the contriver came face to face with times of peace, by worldly seduction, he revived those minds he had overcome in battle by fear of torture.[6] He took away their humility, the only way to tame the anger of an indignant God, and he substituted pride, which he knew for certain would gravely offend God. He promoted the idea that the lapsed, the deserters of heavenly sacraments, could illicitly hold ecclesiastical office again.[7]

As much as he recently took pleasure in their weakness of faith, so now he rejoices in this fraud. He is even more secure when they are called 'bishops' or 'Christians', than when they fell to ruin in their denial of the Christian name. He has these nominal enemies while he remains secure in deception. As we have already said, this is how he holds onto those he deceives by this false use of the Name. Not only does he delight these miserable men with vainglory but he also ensnares the greedy by royal friendship and earthly gifts.[8]

§3   Nevertheless, this rapacious robber was frustrated that he did not control everyone by this ruse. So the enemy of salvation concocted a more subtle conceit to violate the purity of faith. "Christ," he said, "is the lover

---

[6] Those who were wavering, about to abjure their alliance with the *traditores*, were deterred from repenting of their association with them by the prospect of being persecuted for being Donatists.

[7] Donatists did not allow Catholic leaders who joined the Donatist fold to continue to preside over their congregations. They were admitted to the Donatist church as members of the laity. Catholics, on the other hand, recognized pastoral necessity and political prudence in cases where an entire Donatist congregation went over to the Catholic side under the leadership of its priest or bishop. Donatists treated schismatic Donatists returning to their church on a case-by-case basis. Augustine exploited the inconsistencies he perceived in this policy. See A. C. De Veer, "L'exploitation du schisme maximianiste par Saint Augustin dans la lutte contre le Donatisme," *Recherches Augustiniennes* 3 (1965), pp. 219-37.

[8] See Eusebius, *EH* 10.5.15-17 (2.453-55) for the letter of Constantine to Caecilian, bishop of Carthage, on the restoration of church property confiscated during the persecutions before 312.

of unity. Therefore, let there be unity." Those people who were already fawning on him and were deserted by God came to be called 'Catholics'. By prejudice in favor of the name, those who refused to communicate with them were called 'heretics'. He sent funds so that he might weaken their faith or provide an occasion for avarice through the publication of the law.[9] But when the course of justice holds firm and inflexible in the face of these seductive temptations, judges are ordered to intervene; the secular powers are forced to use coercion.[10] Homes are encircled with battle standards; at the same time, threats of proscriptions are launched against the rich. Sacraments are profaned; crowds are bedecked with idolatry; holy assemblies are transformed into splendid banquets.

§4   O most faithful brothers and sisters, it is a crime even to publish what was said and done among the banquets of lascivious youths where despicable women were present.

How swiftly and completely did the situation change! The basilica, shameful to say, was turned into a fast-food restaurant. What grief to see such a crime in the house of the Lord, this place accustomed to pious prayers, now profaned by impure deeds and illegitimate incantations! Now I ask you, what person in whatever desperate condition would allow this to be done in their own home? No one would consent except the sort of person who would actually do it. Who denies that such deeds have the children of the Devil as their authors? Who calls the authors of the actions Christians, except the person who wishes to excuse the Devil himself or to disavow Christ the Lord? What diligence by the Serpent! So many evils let loose! How many hatched so that its family might assume the divine Name and hide itself from that Name, the Name it disgraces by its deeds! O the strength of the divine patience so worthy of praise, bearing up while the villainy of evil is spreading! Divine patience puts up with having the deeds of the crafty enemy imputed to itself or to its Name. Let no one think that something trivial happens when so many schisms and heresies arise. Satan's disguise surely dishonors God and Christ though his wicked

---

[9] See Eusebius, *EH* 10.6.1-5 (2.461-463) for Constantine's letter to Caecilian regarding funds to be distributed to Catholics only.

[10] No copy of the edict of unity has survived. For a discusssion of the events leading up to it and of its enforcement, see Frend, *TDC*, pp. 155-161.

ministry and adulterous work.

§5   But lest we wander too far from the main point, let us omit their defilement of holy virgins. I repress any mention of their slaughter of the priests of God. I keep silent about their assaults, their pillaging, their booty. This way even they may know that we deliberately select few things from among many and we expose it quickly and modestly, seeing that we are eager not to exact vengeance on our enemies but to free the souls of these miserable people from the jaws of the ravenous wolf, indeed from the very mouth of the Dragon (Mt 7.15; cf. Ezek 22.27).

Therefore, the one who corrupts holy discipline could violate the chastity of faith under the by-word of unity, i.e., by compelling unity with himself, not with God. Neither the rulers of this world nor those of darkness arrange things to happen in such a way that what is ordered might reveal the person giving the order. What glorious examples, how many glorious examples of 'the Church of God' or 'the Church of Christ' issue among them? What signs of Christian confession? What exiles, public tokens of true faith and perfect devotion, might there be? By these deeds truth obviously could not lie hidden unless someone in defiance of conscience determined to place their hope in deceit just as the prophet said (cf. Jer 7.4 and 13.25).

§6   Let us proceed to the final events. They erupted in open threats and unmistakable fury once their subterfuges failed and their snares wore out. At that time you could have seen bands of soldiers serving the Furies of the traditors. They were brought together to perform a crime, but they were thinking only of pay. They stood around with most attentive curiosity lest mercenary cruelty be allowed to do something too gently. The cruel mercenaries asserted that attention to so improper a spectacle was not so much defense of a perverse claim, as the exaction of blood according to some contract.

Although the people of God might have anticipated the coming slaughter and known about it from the arrangements being made, they did not flee out of fear of an imminent death. On the contrary, they flew undaunted to the house of prayer with a desire to suffer. There faith grazed on the sacred readings, and prescribed fasts fed them with continual prayers. When these souls are delivered into the hands of the iniquitous, by their prayers they are actually commended into the hands of God (cf. Lk 23.46). Behold, in imitation of the Lord's passion, this cohort of soldiers marshalled by latter-day Pharisees sets forth from their camps to the death of Christians. Against innocent hands stretched out to the Lord, their right hands are armed with cudgels (cf. Mt 26.47). But it may be said that those who are not slaughtered by the sword are no less martyrs for having been beaten to death in this impious massacre.[11]

§7 The sword of the tribune had not yet pierced though the honored throat of the holy bishop of Siciliba,but it pricked him and the rage of the devil revealed who his agents were. In the same way the patience of the glorious bishop revealed the Church of Christ. No one else appears as servant of Christ the Lord as much as someone who suffered the same things as the Lord. It says: "No servant is greater than his master; if they persecute me, they will persecute you (Jn 15.20)." This is why these blind 'servants of God' who are loved by the world show how the Lord himself was 'loved' by the world. If the world does not love even those who are its own, it is necessary for it to hate those whom the Lord Jesus chose from out of the world. It says: "If you were from the world, the world would love what is its own; but because you are not from the world, since I have chosen you from out of the world, for that reason does the world hate you (Jn 15.19)."

§8   Finally, bloodshed marked the end of this hatred. Now the soldiers endorsed the contract and the covenant of crime in no other way than by the seal of blood. Everyone kept their eyes shut tight while each age group and sex was killed, cut down in the midst of the basilica. It is this very basilica, I say, between whose walls so many bodies were cut down and buried. Here, in the inscriptions, memory preserves the name of the persecution as Caecilianist until the end of time, lest after his episcopate the parricide deceive others who were not privy to the things done in his name.

§9   Not without cause then do we celebrate this anniversary with religious devotion, for we must honor this day as the day on which the entire Church of God confessed its faith and was then crowned by the

---

[11] This alludes to the belief that the only true martyrs were those who had actually shed blood. Thus a person beaten to death without the breaking of the skin would be considered less than a martyr. The author obviously repudiates this differentiation among those dying for their faith.

right hand of Christ the Lord, the eternal judge. This day will reflect on how Highest Piety itself did not permit everyone to be butchered here. Scrutinizing the hearts of all, God honors with the reward of the martyrs those whom He saw suffering with the full measure of devotion, for He seeks not the blood but the faith of believers. However, we must hold Caecilian responsible for the blood of all, for we are sure that he arranged for the whole populace to be killed.

§10   Nonetheless, there was an even greater madness: even after so nefarious a deed, the killer thought he could take control of the same basilica, as if she should submit herself to his love for the place.

There were some Christians who escaped. He saw them holding life in this present age as of little value. I suspect he thought that after that gory disgrace when he had sought their blood, after the disaster of the handing over of Scriptures, he had to ingratiate himself with them. So he persecuted those who avoided the contagion of communion with him while he promised indemnification to those who would communicate with him even after he had committed the killings. O imprudence mixed with vanity and madness! This is how the vilest of robbers was blinded. He thought that he had to introduce his plan, but unwittingly he was thwarted by his own arrangements.

§11   Once more then, we must lay before your eyes the violence of his power: now it must be seen, now it must be pondered in the mind. At the same moment when the priest of God is being sacrificed before the altar of the holy Name, in that minute when the young catechumen, not yet privy to a knowledge of the sacraments, now almost dead, most ardently seeks the grace of the saving bath,[12] it says to him, "Come to me." His soul is surely near God now. With his last thirsting gasp he shows that he wishes to partake of this great sacrament so that, just as in the Lord's passion, water might be joined to blood.

§12 But then the renowned bishop came from Avioccala to Carthage. He was received as a 'guest' with the kindness of their 'Catholic' hospitality so that after the fatigue of such a journey he did not even get the chance to drink a sip of water before he himself slaked the thirst of the insatiable gullet of the traitors with a cup of his own blood.

---

[12] I.e., the water of Baptism.

And so, I think we must inquire what sort of apostasy this may be if it is so worthily called 'Catholic'. For as an enemy of the Name, it manages quite well to the enormous detriment of the Name, so that the common people take it as Catholic when they [the Caecilianists] commit without penalty what is censured under common law.

§13　While the tribune had prepared to indulge the wishes of the traitors and an abundance of blood had cooled the heat of their cruelty, some of the brethren entered the basilica again for however much time they could and held funerals for the martyrs. What passion of soul! What groans of lamentation! What devotion! Dashing among the bodies of the massacred, they hurried to identify each of those lying there. When children happened on the bodies of their parents cast upon the ground, and parents on the bodies of their children, you could see some of them holding their dead in their arms. Others half-dead themselves sank down in grief at the unexpected sight. Still others applied their pious hands to the task of collecting the bodies. The bodies of both sexes were touching each other, lying there as would not have otherwise been fitting. Even if they could not give them a proper funeral, they at least returned the limbs to their proper places.

Already the twilight was trying to shut out the light of that day and so right away many bodies were hurriedly brought from the places where they had been scattered. The Spirit was fortifying those who labored piously so that there where the pastor lay transfixed, in that same place the flock of sheep would be gathered round about in their own passion (cf. Mt 23.35). This very fact bore witness from heaven on behalf of their deed: those who offered themselves to God as a sacrifice, by their encircling arrangement, provide a crown for the altar of God. Thus the bishop's funeral rites had indicated his priesthood to the people who attended, and, once he had advanced to martyrdom, he could delight in the company and in the funeral rites of his co-martyrs.[13]

---

[13] This indicates the arrangement of the bodies both of those who were slain on the floor of the church and of those who were later buried in the floor of the church around the bishop, a custom called burial *ad sanctos*. Christians often buried martyrs together under the floors of churches near the altar. The earliest evidence of burial *ad sanctos* comes from *The Acts of Maximilian* 3.4 (Musurillo, p. 249) where the pious woman Pompeiana arranges for the burial of the martyr Maximilian near the grave of Cyprian in 295. Later she herself

§14   O mystery truly divine, so very different from human wisdom! Thus says the Lord through the prophet: "My thoughts are not your thoughts," he says, "nor are my ways your ways: for as far as heaven is from the earth, so far are my ways from your ways, and your thoughts from my understanding (Isa 55.8-9)."

To be slain in the battle line as an adversary of the Gentiles,[14] this is victory; to be killed by the enemy in our combat is triumph. But the murderer who has lived on after his victory is truly a wretched conqueror.

Rejoice and exult, holy mother Church. Instructed in heavenly teachings, you struggle unsullied in a battle for which you cannot be blamed. If you have to resist, you resist with the power of the soul, not with arms; if you fight, it is with faith not force. A multiplicity of battles tests you on earth, crowns you in heaven, and commends you to the Lord Christ. Thus the one conquers who after victory does not know how to be conquered again; thus the one triumphs for whom triumph has no bounds. Only you can fight piously; only you can derive your advantage from the wickedness of others; only you can be crowned with a pure and virgin conscience by Christ. To him be glory and power forever and ever. Amen.

---

was buried near the two men. For a full discussion of the custom, see Yvette Duval, *Auprès des saints corps et âme: L'inhumation 'ad sanctos' dans la chrétienté d'Orient et d'Occident du IIIe au VIIe siècle* (Paris: Études Augustinennes, 1988), especially pp. 52-55.

[14] The identification of the Catholics as Gentiles reinforces the Donatist self-identification as the *collecta*, the assembly of Israel.

THE PASSION OF MAXIMIAN AND ISAAC

INTRODUCTION

The Passion of Maximian and Isaac records the execution of Maximian and the death in prison of his companion Isaac as well as the deaths of others at sea. Section 3 of the text places the events during the second period of the repression of the Donatists, which occurred from 346 to 348. The titulus (bracketed in the translation) dates the execution to August 25th, but the more textually sure date in §12 places the event on August 15th. Section 12 also indicates that some events took place on a day which was coincidentally a Saturday and eighteen before the Kalends of September. Since this coincidence occurred during this period only in 347, the events are dated to that year.[1]

The story is traditionally attributed to Macrobius, a Donatist bishop residing at Rome (perhaps in exile) as late as 366. Its exhortation to martyrdom in §18 would suggest a date of composition between the martyrdom on August 15, 347, and the end of the persecution in 348. This would fit well with the mention of the decree of unity in §3 for this imperial edict reached North Africa in the Spring of 347 and enforcement began in earnest on June 29, 347.[2]

The Passion of Maximian and Isaac is almost formulaic in its descriptions of tortures and in the report of Isaac's dream,[3] but it is distinctive in its record of the event which transpired after the deaths of Maximian and Isaac. The passion tells how prison authorities endeavored to keep the execution of Donatist martyrs from exciting public opinion and from providing relics to be honored. Here we have a focus on the care for the confessors similar to that in the *Acts of the Abitinian Martyrs*. But instead

---

[1] See the calculations in Monceaux 5.86-87 and Maier 1.270.
[2] See Frend, *TDC*, pp. 178-79.
[3] Cf. §§8-9 with *The Passion of Perpetua and Felicitas* §10 (Musurillo, pp. 117-119).

of a Christian bishop interdicting supplies for the bodies of living Christians, this story tells of the removal of the suffering confessors from the reach of the supporting community.

Indeed, the theme harks back to the martyrdom of Polycarp (d. 155/56). Roman officials at Smyrna tried to keep Christians from claiming the body of Polycarp lest they venerate his remains.[4] However, at Carthage prison guards attempted to prevent the collection of relics in a novel way. They prepared a ship and loaded it with imprisoned Donatists *vivi pariter cum defunctis* (the living as well as the dead), along with, no doubt, common criminals. After they sailed out to deep water, they weighted the bodies of the Christians with casks full of sand and dumped the bodies of all the prisoners together into the sea. The officials thought that none of the bodies of the martyrs would wash up on the shore. Even if some of the bodies eventually did, they reasoned, how could the Christians tell the waterlogged and disfigured bodies of the martyrs from those of other prisoners?

But Nature itself cooperated to frustrate the wicked jailers, and the waves separated the bodies of the martyrs from those of the criminals, returning the bodies of the saints to the shore.[5] As in *The Passion of Maxima* §6 where a bear recognized the holiness inherent in the flesh of the martyrs, so here the ocean depths venerate the bodies of the holy ones.

The translation is based on Maier, pp. 259-75. Migne presents two versions by early French patristic scholars, Louis Ellies Dupin (1657-1719) and Jean Mabillon (1632-1707). Dupin's edition (PL 8.767-74) contains notes on variants of a manuscript from Corbie in France. Mabillon's (PL 8.778-84) is only part of the text, from the second paragraph of §5 to the end. Differences between Maier's versions and those of Migne are noted where they are significant for the historical narrative.

The paragraph numbers correspond to the divisions in Maier's edition; Migne has none.

---

[4] See *The Martyrdom of St. Polycarp* §§17-18 in Musurillo, pp. 15-17.
[5] See §§14-16.

TRANSLATION

[Here begins the passion of the holy martyrs Isaac and Maximian, which took place on the seventh before the Kalends of September.[6]]

§1   This is a fitting occasion and I am happy to write to you, brothers and sisters. My zeal for a glorious exhortation along with this outstanding opportunity inflames me. Though I am unworthy to be a witness to the witnesses of Christ, I am writing this letter so that I who am hardly suitable to offer my own account of their martyrdom for the Lord might be allowed to bear witness concerning his martyrs. In short, I would not dare to offer a final word in writing about such martyrs to such an audience except that if I did not announce it to you, I would be jealous with the blameless jealousy of the devoted heart of anyone else who did so.

I know that no one can tell the story better than the person who suffered it or accomplished it. But the one who did not merit either commits a fault only by not making an appropriate report. More likely a person does not take any opportunity to do so unless that person suffered blamelessly whatever they had suffered boldly and joyfully in praise of Christ.

§2   Therefore, I believe it is fitting, sisters and brothers, to consider an example of unsuspected virtue, that is, how the Lord took to heaven the twin martyrs of the church at Carthage, Isaac and Maximian, or simultaneously Maximian and Isaac. I think it is difficult to be able to describe their triumphs in proper order. One can hardly count their earthly commendations much less the heavenly accolades which Christ accorded them. Surely they accomplished the deeds of the entire conflict so quickly that I do not know what came first, second, or third. They combined their greatness and all their glory with such hasty speed they were almost finished before they had begun or, as I should more truthfully say, their deeds came to birth at the same time in both of them. So where shall I begin? At what point shall I open the door of praise and where shall I close it when I leave? I am confused about how to open, and I am vexed about how to close.[7] If I begin by recalling the character of the entire life,

---

[6] August 25th; but see the discussion on dating in the introduction to this story.

[7] This is a common rhetorical opening; see *The Acts of the Abitinian Martyrs* §1.

I shall seem to slight the martyrdom when I come to it. If I digress and go directly to preaching about martyrdom, I shall be considered disdainful of so great a biography because I narrowed my topic. I am urged to recount everything and I know that I cannot do so. The burden of this devout work hems me in on every side, but a saying preserved in the gospel comes to mind as a consolation. A person should have no fear in trying to express this memorial to martyrdom since that person will see the Lord Jesus praising him at the end of his life.[8]

§3   Here at Carthage the savagery of persecution remained dormant in such a way that, while it was in remission for quite a while,[9] it was nourishing even worse trickery. While the enemy was lying in wait everywhere, here alone fears and terrors were keeping silence, so that you might say that the powers of the world had no plans to take action. It excited no venerable ears or hearts. Only the consolation of rumor about your uncounted martyrs of Numidia encouraged the souls of our brothers and sisters.[10] The joy of your glories filled every house as if it were their own, and just as you rejoice today as you would in your own martyrdom. At that time the devil, enraged for a second time, kindled the dying embers of fury into torture and aroused the insane arms of his own violence. But I think he had postponed these activities for quite a while because he had thought that the entire army of Christ had been delivered to him. But when he realized that the Church of the Lord was healthy because of daily exercise, and was growing stronger, right away he felt that he was being made a laughing stock by the errors of his own hope. Stirred up by more horrible incitements, he sought out and chose the heart of a judge suited to himself. Without delay, he made himself subordinate to a proconsul who was his equal in desire. Augmenting the legislation

---

[8] The reference may be to any one of several biblical texts, e.g., Mt 5.10-12, 24.46-47, 25.21; or Jas 1.12.

[9] There is no evidence of systematic persecution of Donatists in Carthage between 321 and 346.

[10] The identity of these martyrs is unknown. The most likely candidate is Donatus of Bagaï who died perhaps during the spring or summer of 347. For the story of bishop Donatus, see Optatus 3.4 (Vassall-Philips, pp. 147-148) and Augustine, *Sancti Aurelii Augustini In Iohannis Euangelium Tractatus CXXIV* 9.15, edited by D. Radbodus Willems, CCSL 36 (Turnhout: Brepols, 1954), p. 120.

of the traitors with his plan of a beastly edict, he immediately ordered a treaty of sacrilegious unity to be solemnly enacted with tortures as sanctions so that those whom Christ commanded to be received for his sake should be perpetually banished (Mt 10.40-42; cf. Jn 13.20) and should not struggle against the treaties of so-called 'unity'. Therefore, tolerating no hindrance to their triumphs, Christ did not permit the sluggards to divide his own army when the enemy challenged them. He immediately chose the hardy soldier Maximian from among the strong men.[11] He made him glorious in this battle, not that the rest were unlike him, but he did it so that the whole war might be exemplified in a single battle. The Lord already knew well from his first confession of faith that he had a lofty disposition.[12] He sent him forth armed with perfect strength, so that what the Lord deigned to show him the day before his passion should not be in vain or ineffectual.

§4   On the previous day,[13] there was a meal with some of the sisters and brothers in the home of a man praiseworthy for Christian sobriety. When Maximian took up the cup as he was about to drink, in fact, right after he had mixed it,[14] immediately a crown lay before his lips, descending into the cup and enclosed within it. Once mixed, it clung to one side or the other and enclosed his reflection. It glimmered with a splendid blood-red color, so that it might appear equally like the blood of his passion and the splendor of his future dignity in heaven. Full of joy at this, he showed this miracle to all who were present and he prayed that they might all join with him in the spirit of love. He wished that whatever happened to him should pertain to all of them. But after he began to drink, in no way was the circlet of the crown broken, but the liquid of the drink grew more concentrated as its quantity was reduced, so that it came to crown internally the soul to which it had come.

Then, on the very next day,[15] relying on such security, he vomited up the excess of the previous day's cup. He seemed to hope for victory in

---

[11] There is no evidence that Maximian was a member of the Roman army. This is a metaphor for service to Christ.

[12] Here is evidence of a previous arrest and release.

[13] August 14th.

[14] It was customary to drink wine mixed with some water.

[15] August 15th.

his very bones, with his lofty disposition tucked deep in a heart which was ready to bear fruit.

§5   But what more can one say? With the speed not of feet but of a well-prepared mind, he quickly sprang up on his own to incite this contest. He scattered the dismal little pieces [of the imperial edict] with his rapid hands just as if he were tearing the devil limb from limb.[16] Immediately he was taken up to the tribunal. By the order of the proconsul and without any delay, he was surrounded by a bestial troop of torturers. From this point on, who could describe the strength of Christ or the savagery of those mangling him, the torturers' punishments or the victories of Christ, the extended insanity of their rage or the constancy of his Christian endurance? The dreadful torturers rose up redoubling their violence in their efforts. They expressed it in the blows of lead-tipped scourges. Bearing in their hands the anger of the judge, they competed in their rage. Who could be found stronger? But opposing them was Christ who was clothed in the limbs of his soldier (cf. Rom 13.14). He turned back from within whatever torments the enraged executioners laid on him from the outside. They tortured him all the more zealously, angry that they inflicted such savagery in vain. And the Lord with his own strength increased his renewed endurance. Fresh guards even more cruel in their madness changed themselves into executioners and the fierce troops so often changed were not enough to commit homicide on one innocent man. On the other hand, the Lord did not desist from changing the constancy of his perseverance into something even better. The vigor of his weighty torture by beating would not have been stopped if he had not also ordered laceration with the rod afterwards. Thus where violent battering had caused swelling, later blows would disclose dislocated joints. The whole body was torn so that this mangling of the limbs created one big wound.

Maximian did not suffer these things passively but he acted like a person estranged from his own body, triumphing over all these tortures. Thus a war was waged between his body and the tortures, between sacrilegious people and a devout man, between strength of soul and

---

[16] I.e., he tore down a copy of the edict which had been posted. See a similar incident in Lactantius, *Of the Manner in which the Persecutors Died* §13 (ANF 7.306).

butchers, between a soldier of Christ and soldiers[17] of the devil, between an enduring person and his judge. One miserable man was enough to fight so gloriously against so much torture and against such a multitude of the enemy that in this one contest, the enemy could not report a single victory. He who went to death in triumph was able to pass the test in his final torment.

But it was proper that he should wait a while for the one whom Christ had assigned as his companion.

§6 For right then renowned Isaac was not restraining his joy at the contest of his associate. He was brought in along with the people of the family of faith[18] on account of his public rejoicing in the Holy Spirit. Full of heavenly endurance, he freely proclaimed, "Come, traitors, recover your insane 'unity'."[19]

At the sound of his voice, the furious proconsul immediately was disturbed enough to ask his staff who was the source of the noise.

But there was no dearth of traitors to lead the way for the soldiers. These very servants of sacrilege hardly had their fill with one victim before handing over another to be sacrificed at their hands in the same way so that they might openly surpass the standards of their ancestors.

Immediately the judge became very angry and had removed the man whom he had tortured just a little while ago. He turned against the second man more violently because he was enraged. He had hardly disposed of one before he became infuriated by the other.

§7 Already drained by the violence, the torturers began the attack again. Cruelty alone made their weary arms stronger now. This squad of executioners repeatedly thirsted[20] for the violence of scourging with their flesh-eating whips and, once they had applied all their strength and exerted all their efforts, they attacked with wailing madness, as if they themselves were suffering what they had inflicted.

What endurance was there in this man as he suffered while the violence

[17] *Milites*: Dupin has *militum*.

[18] Literally, *fraternos populos*.

[19] Dupin's variant from Corbie reads: "Come to the traitors. Satisfy the insanity of your cruelty."

[20] Maier's substitution of *sitiebat* (thirsted) for Dupin's *liciebat* (it was permitted) makes orthographic and narrative sense.

of savage persecution wailed! But the devil was not permitted to overpower the second martyr because it was not right that the victory of Christ which burned bright should cede to anyone in any way. Then after the torture by flogging with a lead-tipped scourge had come to naught, furious barbarity moved them to use switches for flogging,[21] so that the heavenly armor bearers might not differ by any degree of endurance and the enemy might not seem to be tamed because it was using a milder torture.

When the switches were broken and the switch makers had been brought back again and again, Isaac, bearing the name of a victim and imitating the endurance of his namesake (Gen 22.1-19), was tortured. His sworn devotion remained intact. All his joints were broken, the connective tissues torn and moistened,[22] and his voice seemed to echo the proclamation of his confession, finding its exit, so it seemed, from his many wounds. Let no one think that the blows of the switches which followed the mangling by the claws[23] were some sort of mild chastisement, but rather the judge found the claws disgusting. Now there were no lacerations but the interior of the body was revealed. Even the person who had been weakened by these bloody instruments could not say that there had actually been any cutting.[24]

Now the bundle of switches lay idle. They were deprived of their strength almost as if battle axes and pruning hooks had hacked them to pieces. Now the savage assistants panted their weak breaths, wearied by the feeble blows of a defeated ferocity. Yet still their thirsty limbs gazed with eagerness at torments all juicy and waiting to be guzzled down.[25] Then and there Isaac's body scoffed at torments and his mind was filled with joy at their fury and torturing. The one who was racked and condemned by the judge at once obstructed the sentence with no delay, and the judge linking both in an equal destiny bound them over for exile. As soon as they had been thrust into prison, Isaac immediately brought to

---

[21] Mabillon omits the switches, *virgas*.

[22] The moisture would not have been blood, as later information reveals, but synovial fluid, the transparent liquid which lubricates the joints.

[23] For the nature of these claws, see *The Acts of the Abitinian Martyrs* §5.

[24] Note the reluctance of the torturers to actually shed blood and therefore provide the Donatists with 'martyrs'; cf. *The Passion of Donatus*, n. 11.

[25] Cf. *The Acts of the Abitinian Martyrs* §10.

completion the attainment of his martyrdom; and what is more, at the same time, he abandoned all his prisons, both his body and the world, lest the revelation of his vision have been mistaken in any way. Thus he went through everything in correct order so that what would happen seemed to have happened already in that vision.

§8   For when he was held just a little by deep sleep, it seemed to him that he had a battle with the assistants of the emperor, not for any reason, of course, except that for which he endured his passion. And clearly it was nothing but proof of his devotion that what he considered his ardent desire while he was awake, he would suffer even in his sleep. Thus he brought to fulfillment what the Prophet testified concerning him: he says, "I sleep and my heart keeps watch (Cant 5.2)." His devotion then kept watch, engaged in the struggles of virtue, and he boldly beat back the assistants of wickedness who were fighting him under orders from the king. When he had overcome them after a long battle, suddenly he caught sight of the emperor himself also approaching: while he was being urged by the emperor to follow his order, he denied the authority of the sacrilegious order and of the fierce torture threatening him. With repeated threats, the dreadful man also promised that he would pluck out his eyes too. Since they had fought each other savagely for a long time in these battles, Isaac would not countenance simply being declared the winner, but laying hold of the emperor aggressively, he ended the delay to his threats. Violently jerking up the eye, he emptied the socket, leaving behind a face bereft of its eye.

§9   Next a man of resplendent brilliance appeared rejoicing in Isaac's victory and immediately placing a radiate[26] crown on his head. The faces of his many brothers and sisters seemed fixed on the rays of the crown. Rejoicing he handed it over to him as a reward, and laughing, he made sport of his adversary with strong reproaches. Then the enemy, driven by strong vexation, ordered Isaac to be tortured with savage torment so that he might take revenge for his own torment. But already the victor, Isaac perceived that he was carried upward by the hands of bearers and that he was lifted up, flying more quickly to the heights of heaven. While he was happily on his way, he heard a voice from above, like that of an

---

[26] The *corona radiata* was an iconographic statement of the divinization of the wearer.

old man, shouting, "Woe to you, world, for you are perishing!" (Cf. Rev 18.10, 16 and 19; and 1 Cor 7.31). After this rang out three times, he came to the climax of his vision and thereafter he accomplished what he had seen.

§10   What could be plainer than this vision? What could be expressed more clearly when it was arranged in chronological order? Now just as he had observed himself fighting with the ministers of the king all alone in the night, so later during the day he embodied this for us. As he had plucked out the eye of the emperor, so he had blinded him by conquering him. As he had won the prize of a crown so was he crowned publicly. As he saw many faces fixed on rays of his crown, so all the people kept watch at his passion. So he flew to heaven, just as he merited coming to martyrdom quickly. Only this has yet to happen: he had prophesied annihilation for the world and we all know he was not lying.

§11[27] Now would anyone among the sisters and brothers by chance become frightened and declare that Maximian was not the equal [of Isaac] because, having confessed earlier, he was held back, outliving Isaac for a short time? Perish the thought, brothers and sisters, that they might be divided[28] for they fought in equal battles! If the Lord by a financial arrangement made equal those coming into the vineyard at different times (Mt 20.1-16), how would one judge them unequal when they were found laboring at the same time? But because Isaac seems to die earlier, how much more do I say that the Lord makes them equal: as the former suggested to the latter an inducement to confess, thus did the latter induce the former equally to the crown [of martyrdom]. The Lord wished both of them to be teachers for each other so that he might make them equal in their reciprocal influence of patterning. Lest one surpasses the other, the one seems to conform to the other in every way. Now truly both precede each other; both follow each other.[29]

§12   But meanwhile a ship was being prepared for exile for those

---

[27] Following a change in subject matter, Maier inserts a break after the end of the previous sentence. Migne's versions continue the sentence immediately.

[28] Mabillon has *videantur*, seen instead of *dividantur*.

[29] The quandary of the community whether those who die later are worthy of more praise is reflected an earlier Carthaginian story, *The Martyrdom of Marian and James* §8.7-8 (Musurillo, p. 206), where the answer was in the negative.

confined in prison: I believe this was not arranged by any human plan. It was obvious that it was provided by heavenly aid. The Lord wanted them to be brought to their end within the space of one day, so that just as in the vision of the martyr, they might be honored through the vigils of the people, for[30] when Isaac died he was a messenger[31] filling the ears of all [with the news] concerning the accomplishment of his martyrdom. The entire community of faith speedily hurried on their joyful way to his corpse. When the burial of his body was denied to them by his executioners, they all held vigils there with great rejoicing during the entire day lest the body be thrown out unburied. At night the exulting people proudly[32] sang psalms, hymns, and canticles in testimony. Every age and sex rejoiced with ardent desire to attend such festivities of thanksgiving. What kind of honor is this, sisters and brothers, that the Lord judges fit to procure for his martyrs, so that on the eighteenth day before the Kalends of September, on a Saturday, just like at Easter, the people might be permitted to celebrate a vigil! In that way the days were filled and the nights consumed.

Then when the next day had dawned,[33] they waited to see what the proconsul would order concerning the burial of the body. Perhaps the wretch might assent to what was not normally denied to either homicides or adulterers. On the other hand, the traitors' cruel destructiveness[34] might stay alert to keep the counsels of cruelty. Then goaded by their suggestion, the proconsul ordered the people who had been assembled to be expelled from the prison, and the living as well as the dead to be dumped into the billows of the sea, so that they would not be permitted to reverence the dignity of the martyrs.

§13   How stupid the cruelty which wished to deny our hands their bodies, as if it could take their veneration from our minds. As if by not being buried in the earth, they could not otherwise enter into the heavenly kingdom! But something happened to add to the evidence of their happi-

---

[30] *Nam*; Mabillon has *non*, not, here.

[31] Nuntius; Dupin has *notius*, an awkward construction and probably a scribal error.

[32] Instead of *gloriose*, Mabillon has *gloriae domini*, to the glory of the Lord.

[33] Sunday, August 16th, 347. On the dating to the year, see n. 1.

[34] For *pernicies*, Corbie and Mabillon have *protinus*, immediately.

ness: after their earthly tortures for the sake of Christ, even the dead
might be shaken by their trials at sea. In that way there might be no place
on earth where they had not mocked the enemy.

The Lord provided this situation for them to amass more triumphs. Thus
they might labor subject to an even greater hatred by the world and so
be able to show forth power in their bodies whether living or dead.
Therefore, the soldiers[35] and the senior guards, armed with clubs, came
to the prison, and driving the people from that road to slaughter, they
wounded almost all of them. So much had to be attributed to the dignity
of the martyrs that for the sake of their burial others too merited to make
a confession.[36] Afterwards they had hardly been able to remove them.
An unequal number of soldiers on each side led out the dead equally with
the survivors.

Pointless cruelty unwittingly deceived itself so that it might supply the
very funeral rites to those to whom it had otherwise denied them! Now
they approached the shore of the sea, now the ship carried the martyrs
on board so that it might submerge them. As swiftly as it reached deep
water, no less zealously did the retinue of Satan rush to fulfill their orders.
Then they sent them off,[37] one at a time with quite a long time between
them. They were bound by ropes. Each one was tied neck and feet to two
casks filled with sand. The weight pulled them down.

§14   When the sea recognized those thrown into its lap, immediately
it glistened all over with heavenly flames. It could not hold the most holy
limbs. So the waves rolled from top to bottom and the sea washed away
the sand it had dislodged, exposing their bodies. Turning back, it moved
them from the depths to the surface with its retreating waves. Descending
to the bottom, the searching waves plunged down from the surface
swirling to the depths with tremendous force. At the right moment the sea
was driven back by a stronger eddy. It was compelled to bring forth the
limbs of the saints and the vortex of the waves discharged the submerged
bodies with a rapid torrent of force. The victorious surge, drawing up its

---

[35] Mabillon has *cuncti milites*, all the soldiers.

[36] Those who visited the martyrs in jail will receive similar honor for their bodies will
suffer similar ignominies. See §§14-15.

[37] For *dimiserunt*, Corbie has *demerserunt*, they sank them.

immense weight, finally left behind the bodies it had captured. Then banks of water were raised more forcefully like substantial mountains so that the accumulated mass might bear upwards its burden of bodies so they would not suffer being overwhelmed again. A vault was formed in the sea and the wave battled on all sides with its own weight under the unified mass of water so that it would not expose the sea bottom to the heavy weight of the water.[38]

§15   But there was still one more task left to accomplish, the struggle for the sea to gather together[39] into a lively congregation those who had been dispersed over a vast distance lest due to its negligence, the sacrilege committed by another might survive. The waters tugged here; the rising whorls swelled there with double crests. The sea immediately brought back the bodies conveyed to it for a proper reunion.[40] Their approach began to shorten the distance between the crests, and as they came closer to the midpoint, the decreasing length of the space between both crests reached the critical point. When the whole distance disappeared once and for all, the entire interval vanished and all of the space between them disappeared. At the very same time that everything was restored to its former condition, the meeting of waves and bodies was celebrated.

§16   Then the beaches were occupied by the brothers and sisters, as if some report preceded the martyrs as they were approaching. For days and nights during that time, they anxiously strained their eyes[41] and hoped for what they believed would happen. They waited for the time to come as it always did with the help of God. Then suddenly, after twice three days,[42] they rejoiced at the appearance of the temples of Christ (cf. 1 Cor 6.19) and everyone ran however they could. With joy filling their eyes, they fixed their gaze. The waves crashing with joy handed over to

---

[38] For *terram contingeret aperire*, Mabillon has *terga contingere aperiret*, so as not to expose their backs.

[39] Mabillon adds *in quinquies*, perhaps, "by fives".

[40] For *coitione* Mabillon has *cohibitione*, restraint.

[41] For *monumenta defixis obtunitibus*, Mabillon has *praemonita defixis oppantibus*: they were kept alert by their customary beliefs.

[42] Mabillon adds *ad exemplum umere scilicet geminatim*: just like the doubling of the back. Perhaps the addition should have read *humere . . . germinatum*: sprouting from the earth (cf. John 12.24 and Tertullian, *Apology* 50 [ANF 3.55]).

their outstretched arms the bodies they had waited for, marked with signs
of victory. The community of faith, committed as they were to this
common devotion, received them with glad embraces.

Thus the blessed martyrs received the interment due them. The sisters
and brothers provided the burial rites for which they all had hoped.[43]
Thus Christ discredited the ineffectual plans of the traitors. He would not
permit the bodies of such people to remain unburied and he would not
defraud the devotion of the people in any way, nor would he watch
unmoved as the impious fulfilled their vows of cruelty with their blasphemy of his name.

§17   Now let the mad rage of the scoundrels sound its cry, that rage
which did not wish to recognize the Lord's help. It did not fear that he
would be able to deliver bodies from the sea, when they knew he could
even snatch souls from the nether world. Since the monster who vomited
would not swallow anything more (Jon 1.17-2.10), wretched cruelty lost
out because it believed that it had found a great plan, a plan from which
the sea itself was not willing to withhold consent.[44] It ineptly entrusted
its desires [to the sea] for it [the sea] had no desire to oppose its creator.
What does human madness now accomplish when the sea does not
prosecute the martyrs?[45] What does the savagery of criminals accomplish
when the wild seas recover them for burial? What kind of people, condemned by the persecutors, did the elements fear to injure? O memorable
glory of the blessed passion in which Christ deigned to display so many
wonders! O happy death which came to such as these! Their merits
distinguished them by so many manifestations of his power: constancy in
devotion, endurance in suffering, victory in death, and a miracle[46] in
their burial.[47]

§18   Now, brothers and sisters, all these conditions which led them[48]
to the heavenly kingdom come round to you. These exemplars compel

---

[43] Maier amends the text to read *rediderunt fratres*. The manuscripts have *rediderunt
fratribus*: they provided burial rites for the brothers and sisters.

[44] Maier needlessly changes *nec negare potuit* to *nec negare noluit*.

[45] For *martyres* Mabillon has *mortuos*, the dead.

[46] Instead of *miraculum* Corbie has *mirabilis*, wonder.

[47] For a similar list of virtues, see *The Acts of The Abitinian Martyrs* §1.

[48] For *eos* Maier substitutes *vos*, you.

you. This situation drove them on first to these glories for your sake. The multitude of your own confessions made you teachers through your oft-repeated professions of faith. Now *they* advise *you* concerning martyrdom. Your pattern which encouraged others likewise now encourages you. Now they are holding out their arms to you from heaven, waiting for the time when they will run to meet you. Hurry earnestly;[49] run persistently. They are waiting to take up their place of honor right along with you. Come on, do it, sisters and brothers. Hurry, the sooner the better, so that we may rejoice in the same way over you. May our return find among you a reason for boasting just as our departure from these things shared the joys of glory. When it comes to these affairs, our emulation is a share in the joys of your glory. But let us arrive, coming to you in your triumphs. Just as we have announced their victories to you, so will yours be announced here at Carthage to all the rest who succeed you.

[Here ends the letter of the blessed martyr Macrobius to the people of Carthage about the passion of the martyrs Isaac and Maximian. Thanks be to God. Amen.][50]

---

[49] For *grauiter*, Mabillon has *nauiter*, diligently.
[50] Mabillon adds the bracketed materials.

THE MARTYRDOM OF MARCULUS

INTRODUCTION

Shortly after the promulgation of the imperial edict of unity, on June 29, 347, a group of Donatist bishops met with personal representatives of the emperor, the imperial notaries Paul and Macarius, at Vegesela.[1] Heading the delegation was Bishop Marculus. The discussion did not go well and the bishops were taken into custody. Marculus was retained while the others were eventually released after torture. He was marched from place to place and finally executed at Nova Petra on November 29, 347.

The method of Marculus' execution, being thrown from a cliff by Roman soldiers, is unique among extant Donatist martyrologies. The rumor of Donatist self-martyrdom by precipitation was circulated by Catholics ridiculing Donatism. They claimed that when Roman persecutions ceased in 321, Donatists were frustrated in their attempts to achieve their martyrs' crowns, so many of them simply committed suicide. Sometimes that was accomplished by attracting attention to themselves, claiming to be Donatists and goading others to murder them. Failing other attempts, they jumped from cliffs. Stories circulated of Donatist women vowed to celibacy who preferred self-precipitation to forced marriage.[2] In a parody of these rumors that Donatists martyred themselves by jumping off mountainsides, Marculus was pushed over the edge of the precipice. Whether Marculus committed suicide or was murdered, the Donatists

---

[1] This is the site of a monument to the martyred bishop. See Lancel, SC 373.1518.

[2] See the story of Secunda who jumped from her balcony to avoid marriage and to join Maxima and Donatilla on their way to martyrdom in *The Passion of Maxima* §4. See also the endorsement of Victoria's self-precipitation from a cliff to avoid marriage in *The Acts of the Abitinian Martyrs* §17.

treasured the *passio* within their community.[3]

The translation is based on PL 8.760-766 which Maier reproduces. Migne used the text given in Mabillion with several reading from an otherwise unidentified fourteenth-century manuscript from Corbie. Section numbers of the translation correspond to the unnumbered paragraphs in Migne and the divisions in Maier.

TRANSLATION

§1   Here begins the Passion of the blessed Marculus which took place three days before the Kalends of December.[4]

The passions and the glories of many martyrs have already been laid out in lofty style as a sublime memorial. They provide great benefit for the people who listen each time they are recited as an incentive to virtue and as praise for the Church. For this reason, the honor of such a martyr and an increase in the common devotion of all incited me also that I too, unworthy yet full of love, might expound in an oration the *passio* of the glorious Marculus, radiant with priestly honor, brought to perfection only recently through the shameful crime of the traitors. It is right and proper enough that the bravery of the more recent martyrs should be joined to the praise of the witnesses of old.[5] The rage of the Gentiles[6] who were obeying the devil chose the martyrs for the heavenly kingdom; and so the savagery of the traitors who were serving the Antichrist sent them to heaven.

We must not omit the memorable course of his earlier life. Even if no

---

[3] Optatus 3.6 (Vassall-Phillips, p. 152) claimed that Marculus was killed. Augustine knew the Catholic story of Marculus as suicide as well as the Donatist report of martyrdom, but he made no certain judgment. See *Contra Cresconium* 3.49.54 (CSEL 52.461), *Contra Litteras Petiliani* 2.20.46 (CSEL 52.46) and *In Iohannis Euangelium* 9.15 (CCSL 36.120).

[4] I.e., November 29, 347.

[5] Here is an echo of the approbation of contemporary martyrs as in *The Martyrdom of Perpetua and Felicity* §1 (Musurillo, p. 107), but without the latter's eschatological urgency.

[6] The Donatists cast themselves as the faithful, the new Israel, in contrast to their persecutors. See *The Acts of the Abitinian Martyrs* §22 and their use of the word 'assembly' (*collecta*) in §1 and *passim*.

one can count all the virtues of the glorious Marculus because of their great number, one must speak of at least a few items on account of their testimony.

§2   He had been selected and predestined by the Lord. When he received his first instructions in the faith, he immediately repudiated worldly education. His mind was caught up to heaven and he rejected his legal profession and the false dignity of secular learning. Transferring from the fraud-filled quarters of the magistrates to the most holy school of the Church, he chose the true Teacher, Christ.[7] Thus he merited being honored among the foremost disciples of Christ. What an upright conscience he had, what innate modesty of outstanding character, what spiritual charm in his appearance! I do not think that I have to work hard here: the fact that he merited the priesthood gives approbation to his earlier life. Truly the way he exercised his priesthood is demonstrated by this: the Lord gave him martyrdom as a reward.

§3   Accordingly, he passed his life in a praiseworthy manner in the duties of the heavenly precepts. After he had been designated *summus pontifex*[8] with other holy men, he exercised his own good priesthood. But then suddenly, vicious rumblings of the Macarian persecution thundered forth from the tyrannical home of king[9] Constans and from the pinnacle of his palace. Two beasts were sent to Africa, *viz.*, the same Macarius and Paul. In short, an accursed and detestable war was declared against the Church, so that the Christian people would be forced into unity with the traitors, a unity effected by the unsheathed swords of soldiers, by signals given by the standard bearers[10] and by the shouts of crowds. But

---

[7] The journey of the believer from traditional Roman religion through philosophy and the law or rhetoric is a popular motif in conversion narratives, e.g., Justin, *Dialogue of Justin, Philosopher and Martyr, with Trypho, A Jew* §2-3 in ANF, Vol. 1: *The Apostolic Fathers, Justin Martyr, Irenaeus*, translated by A. Cleveland Coxe, pp. 195; and in a more complex manner in Augustine's *Confessions*.

[8] I.e., bishop.

[9] Naming Constantine as 'king' rather than 'emperor' or 'augustus' adds to the opprobrium, as the title 'king' was used from the time of the Roman republic as the designation for a tyrannical ruler.

[10] Literally *draconum*, of the dragons. This term would remind those who heard the story of the intimate association of the traitors and the *Draco*, the Devil.

while Macarius, the more fearsome of the two beasts, had for a long time carried on this bloody business in the rest of the provinces in an under-handed way, however, in Numidia, he made public charges against the renowned Marculus of barbarous cruelty and unheard of ferocity.

At that time the most holy assembly of aged fathers and a united council of priests sent to him ten of their number, seasoned bishops, as their legates, to dissuade him from such a crime by their wholesome admoni-tions, or at least, as indeed it happened, to become the very first to spring forth into the field of most devout combat and to the battle line of faith.[11] The duty of the noble pastors was directed from heaven so that whatever cruelty might threaten the sheep should first tear at their own limbs.

§4   The most holy Marculus came among these. When the bishops found Macarius on a certain estate called Vegesela, they were immediately received by the man who in his refinement presided over the sacrilegious unity. The priestly limbs of each of the bishops were stripped and each one was bound to a column so that they might collapse under harsh blows by cudgels. Now who could tell of the perseverance of the glorious Marculus? Who might prevail by virtue of eloquence in displaying the unheard of rage of his persecutors or the astonishing defense by Christ the Lord exhibited in the martyr? Because of this, savage ferocity was excited against him with even harsher rage so that hatred of this soon-to-be martyr might now rouse the devil, and the villainy of the precursor to the Antichrist might not be concealed from the Holy Spirit. When he could no longer withstand Marculus' soul strengthened by divine constancy, he fought a battle of pain through the frailty of Marculus' body.

Then when bloodthirsty bands of robbers surrounded the bravest soldier of Christ, the barbaric army of soldiers immediately was transformed into executioners.[12] When they tried to tie him to a column with rough ropes, at once he seized the occasion to display the power of God. Without being asked, he fastened the fetters on his arms and the bonds on his fingers to a column, so that no punishment could tear him away, no cruelty could separate him from it. By this deed the persecutors knew that the servant

---

[11] Cf. the military rhetoric of *The Acts of the Abitinian Martyrs*, especially in §§1, 3 and 4.

[12] Cf. *The Martyrdom of Maximian and Isaac* §5 for a similar scenario.

of God for the sake of God's name yearned for tortures more than he feared them and that someone could not feel the pains of torture in the body when the spirit embraces Christ and hope already possesses the kingdom.

§5   So it happened that a great number of executioners raged against a single man. Wearing out his sacred limbs with the harsh punishment of their cudgels, they mangled him with their torture and with their torment. As much as they inflicted blows on his back with such punishment, so much did the hardness of the column pound on his chest. Cruelty struck every part of his body, but the mouth of the noble man brought forth nothing but praise for God (cf. Pss 36.30 and 50.17). Rage was out of breath: now savagery was overcome by the perseverance of the suffering man and the weariness of the torturers. At this point then, Christ, arrayed in the limbs of the martyr (cf. 1 Cor 6.15), unveiled a miracle: not only did he not allow pain to touch Marculus, but he even stripped from his body all signs of rage and all marks of torture. The enemy was conquered and subdued in this battle. Not content with the cruelty of its punishment, the enemy destined him for a more horrible--or so it seemed to them--sentence and a most well-known passion.

Next they dragged him with them through the other cities of Numidia as some sort of public spectacle of their cruelty which unwittingly provided amazement for the Gentiles, confusion to the enemies of Christ, and an incentive to glorious combat to the servants of God.

§6   But truly, as soon as the enemy had devised an exquisite and grim form of death, it immediately led him with them under a strict guard of soldiers to the citadel of Nova Petra which is situated near the precipice of a steep mountain by the same name. There the Lord filled his martyr with such happiness, he granted him so much joy over his approaching passion, that the span of four days during which he had to wait for his impending crown already had to be numbered not among the hardships of worldly affliction but among the triumphs of the heavenly kingdom. How much could he exult! After a wearisome sojourn in the flesh and in the world, once his journey was over, he hastened to see God and Christ. Travelling as he was to the company of angels and the embrace of the saints, he passed over the very threshold of paradise.

§7   He prayed constantly and continually. His contemplation was unlimited in devotion. He kept the gospel in his speech and martyrdom in his thoughts. He was as devoted to heavenly virtues in his speech as he was in his feelings. He brought forth from his mouth what he had borne enclosed in his heart. Still thirsting for spiritual justice (Mt 5.6) and totally devoted to serving a deserving God, he ended the last of his four days fasting so that when the Sunday dawned in which his passion was to be perfected, the devoted soul of the priest might be made more acceptable to God in offering a double sacrifice.[13] Thus the great high priest was a stranger not only to the enticing world, but even, in fact, to its food. Truly, in approaching the altars of Christ to place on them offerings, he himself was worthy to become an offering for Christ.

Finally, as much as he was able to fast in the presence of the Lord, so much did he evoke the presence of Christ in himself by that purification. Because of this, the reward for his passion was shown to him in a heavenly revelation even before it happened.

§8 The greater part of the night had passed and dawn had arrived. People think this is the best time for prayer and for all religious affairs because the hour is joined to the day as it is being born while all human affairs and business are still at rest. Therefore, at that time, the priest, rising to celebrate the sacraments, was not so much cleansed by sleep as roused to prayer to God by the joy of his recent vision. Before he had begun the mysteries, to the delight of his brethren who were present, he began a faith-filled sermon about what had been shown to him from on high.

"I saw," he said, "these three gifts offered to me from the eternal treasury of the bountiful Lord: a cup made from the brightest silver, a crown shining with glittering gold, and the most sublime palm branch which, full of joy, provided the complement of the forenamed emblems of triumph."

Brethren, the Lord showed a great pledge of imminent glory to the martyr. He revealed a great truth concerning him and his future honor. Nothing seemed obscure or ambiguous in this revelation in which he took the cup which he would have to drink in his passion, in which he took up the crown which was owed to him when his martyrdom was completed, and in which he merited the palm, hoping through this victory that he

---

[13] The Eucharist and martyrdom.

might be secure from attack in the contest.

§9   After this incident, he completed the religious rites as was the custom. Some moments of the night still remained when suddenly the ever-watchful messenger of villainy arrived with the savage orders of Macarius. He bore the unambiguous sentence of most cruel death; he brought to completion the innumerable glories of the martyr and the detestable crime of the persecutors. When the office of the guard had unlocked the doors previously closed to him and acknowledged to him what their very early arrival had brought, their hearts were immediately transformed to lamenting. O how great was the grace of that man! How pervasive the love all around him! How all-encompassing the desire that, through his passion, even the cruelty and martial rigor of the guards might be moved to pious tears! Amidst the weeping and emotions of all, he alone persevered unshaken as he rejoiced that the hour of his death was approaching. He could not be disturbed or sad for he was the one whom faith had made joyful and divine revelation had made calm.

§10   Then, because the rest were afraid, one of the number of those soldiers, the most repulsive executioner, he who alone had been prepared by the devil to bring about the death of this distinguished man, anticipated the deed in his speech. He began to explain the martyrdom in detail to all who listened. He himself had seen it in some sort of dream. "When I was being held by the quiet of the night, suddenly I saw you appearing to me as if you were tied with rough bonds and utterly weighed down by heavy ropes. Then I untied the ropes with my own hand. Because of this, hope for mercy and for a pardon to be followed by your release."

It was not an absurd dream, an incongruous vision, which the executioner saw. Not without cause did he repeat what he had seen. But he followed the example of the impious Caiaphas who when he was about to kill the Lord prophesied about his passion (cf. Jn 11.49-52). Rightly now had he seen the martyr tied up. He who up to now was stationed in a corporeal dwelling, in the double prison of the world and the body,[14] was bound by the difficulties of temporal life. For a person feels the bonds of the body, feels the prison of the world, when troubled by trials. So not without some logic had the executioner dreamt that he had untied him.

---

[14] Cf. *The Passion of Maximian* §7 for the motif of the double prison.

By those cruel hands Marculus had to be separated from his body with the help of death. After the weightiest bonds of worldly oppression, he was about to make a journey through his passion to the freedom of the heavenly kingdom. When we are freed from this world and hurry to the Lord, we are released from heavy bonds. The Apostle demonstrates this when he says: "It seems much better to be released and to be with Christ (Phil 1.23)." For by similar reasoning the most just Simeon pointed this out, aroused by the certainty of his approaching death. He rejoiced that he would be able to escape the troubles of this world. He said: "Now, O Lord, you dismiss your servant in peace, for my eyes have seen your salvation (Lk 2.29-30)." He never would have borne witness that he was to be dismissed with every joy unless he held his bodily condition as some sort of bondage.

§11   Then no delay, no span of time came to pass before the most cruel executioner attacked as in a predawn robbery, to bring to pass what he had already seen. Immediately turning hostile, he urged that the witness of God be brought forth from custody and be led to the rugged heights of the natural rock, a precipice of rough stone. The bloodthirsty and barbaric exactor of profane 'unity'--and the cruelty of the traitors accursed for all ages--chose this harsh mode of death. The glorious Marculus left the building surrounded by a squad of guards and a division of soldiers, honored even by his persecutors. He left resolute in the constancy of his Christian virtue, leaving behind the hotel of humanity, hurrying on to the abode of angels. He left joyful in appearance, accelerating his pace, thinking not so much of the present punishment as of future glory. He was led along the road to the sacrifice which had been prepared for him. Banks of earth were built up on both sides, piles of stone rising little by little. He arrived at the summit notorious for his passion. The very nature of the mountain made itself useful, so that first treading the lower slopes of the hill, then the lofty heights, as if he were mounting up to the top by some sort of steps, he approached heaven and the stars in his body itself. Thus while he was still in this world, he was higher than the world. Whatever seems valuable, whatever lofty in this world, he rejoiced to throw under the soles of his feet.

When he had ascended to the very summit of the rock, all the soldiers pulled back, some from fear, some from distress, and they kept their distance from the singularity of the crime. Even if they were present with guilty fear, they did not want to be involved in the deed.

§12   Then the savage executioner with a double dose of cruelty, there on the precipice, armed with a sword, wielded a double death with his hands. He hurled the martyr downward with his cruel right arm. He believed that he had thrown into the dark depths the man owed the heights of heaven. In fact, once the solidity of the earth was removed, Marculus' body, descending from on high to the depths, was borne through the empty expanse of liquid air. Not finding anything to strike against in that void, he doubled the speed of his progress with a rapid plunge. The swiftness and duration of the fall fostered a tumbling through the rushing rustle of the agitated air. The moderation of his speed was managed from on high so that his limbs, exempt from all adversities, might be placed atop the harshness of the rocks as if on the softest bed or the calmest waves. Then his victorious soul by its natural progress sought heaven more swiftly than his body had descended to earth; so with his own passion completed, both entities should be returned to the ancient sources of their origin[15] by the hands of the omnipotent God who kindly cared for the totality of the martyr. He ordered that his spirit should be placed in its eternal dwelling place by the assistance of the angels and that his intact body, encircled by caressing breezes, supported by gently assisting winds, should be laid at the center of the base of the rocks.

§13   The exquisite schemes of the persecutors and the evil counsels of the traitors were brought into disarray by the help of Christ. They had planned on such a punishment as this so that the memory of the martyr might never be honored by the people of God in their testimony. For they erroneously thought that the body might be mangled on the precipice, that it might be torn by the sharp-edged rocks, so that the one deprived of life might not even have need for burial. They thought that nothing could even arrive at the ground which the pious fraternity might collect and bury,

---

[15] This is testimony to the belief that everything in the world was composed of four elements, earth, air, water and fire, in various proportions. The system, advanced by Empedocles and later by Plato, included the belief that when the bonds holding an entity dissolved and that entity returned to its constitutive elements, each of those elements would seek reunion with the element whence it came. Since the body was composed primarily of earth and the soul primarily of air, the former naturally descended to the earth and the latter ascended to the sky.

since each of the limbs might be held in the recesses of the high mountain or the entire body might be swallowed up all at once in some cleft in the fissures of the rocks or in the fractured recesses of the cliffs. But look! The hard stones and rough rocks spared his consecrated limbs. The mountains feared to harm the man whom the traitors did not fear to slay. Except for those people, every creature adores its creator and in this respect the mountains could not lack the capacity to deserve God's favor. Even Scripture gives them a voice for his praise (Ps 148.9; Dan 3.75).

§14 Meanwhile, the fact that the glorious Marculus had achieved blessed victory in his struggle was concealed within the individual recollections of the soldiers. So in the silence of the night they brought the crime to its conclusion so secretly that not even in the fortress in which he was guarded could outsiders or the brethren have known about it, had not divine help and heavenly signs disclosed what had happened. For as soon as entry of the dawning of the day poured into the pale light of the orb of the night, and the dissimilarity of the dark and the light changed the variously colored face of heaven, immediately a magnificent cloud appeared at the center of the base of the mountain. While lightning flashed, the cloud bore witness concerning the body of the martyr with its caressing light. That cloud heavy with morning dew failed to throw any shadow like a dark cover on the vividly colored hills, but all aglow it wrapped his auspicious limbs with a bright fleecy cover. While human ceremonies might have been omitted just then, in a way the cloud seemed to take the place of a shroud. Meanwhile, the cloud was occasionally pierced by bright lightning and it glimmered through the winding clefts so that by wondrous mighty feats it might alert the ignorant about his passion, or, because the darkness of the night still hung over the area, it might show those who were piously searching a way to find the body.

§15 Therefore, the excitement of the association of believers[16] flamed bright, kindled by these admirable works of God, and suddenly the entire area resounded with a ringing shout, and they declared to each other their common commitments in their pious scurrying to and fro. People of both sexes equally and of every age left their homes in a hurry and flew to the mountain and the cloud in their longing for the martyr. Neither the

---

[16] Literally, *fraternitas*.

impairment of old age nor the weakness of youth nor the fragility of sex could hold back any soul from that place. The ardor of their common faith set them all aflame. As the scurrying throng had come to those places which lay beneath the precipice, their common purpose in running had brought them together into one crowd; then their concern for finding the body dispersed them over the whole mountain. There you could see the duties of piety divided up among the people. Some with impulsive hands explored the briar patch with its rough stalks; others cast their eyes as witnesses into the crooked crevices in the gaping rocks; still others went back over the rocks they had already looked behind with their anxious eyes, lest their haste make fools of them. In the end, because their search could not be successful without the Lord, lightning was sent to that place to reveal the location which they were all seeking. The radiance of the cloud served as an indicator to point out the body longed for by the brethren. On that spot what weeping mixed with all their joy! What embraces round his distinguished limbs! At last when with difficulty they were all satisfied, funeral rites were celebrated with great joy by the brethren and the honor of a religious burial was restored with the greatest jubilation. For the glory of his name, the Lord revealed everything that the enemy had tried to conceal.

§16   O the memorable and extraordinary martyrdom of blessed Marculus! O the example of unshaken virtue eagerly sought by all the devout! O the exemplar necessary for all the ranks of the clergy, by which he came to the palm, the reward of his praiseworthy life! He renounced the world in his catechumenate, showing himself worthy of the priesthood as a neophyte. In his priesthood the office of martyrdom was honored, in his martyrdom a testimony to the power of the Divine. To whom be honor and glory and power forever and ever. Amen.

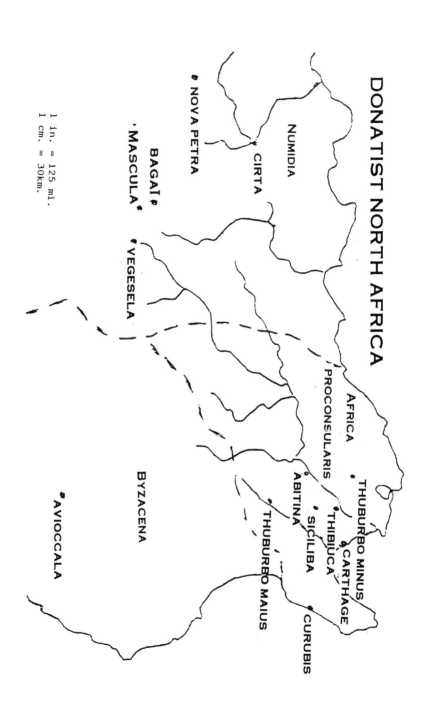

DONATIST NORTH AFRICA

1 in. = 125 mi.
1 cm. = 30km.

NOVA PETRA

NUMIDIA

CIRTA

BAGAÏ
MASCULA

VEGESELA

AFRICA
PROCONSULARIS

THUBURBO MINUS

CARTHAGE

THIBIUCA

SICILIBA

ABITINA

CURUBIS

BYZACENA

THUBURBO MAIUS

AVIOCCALA

BIBLIOGRAPHY

I. Texts and Translations of Stories in this Volume

A. Individual stories

The Acts of Saint Felix Bishop and Martyr: La Passion de S. Felix de Thibiuca. Edited by Hippolyte Delehaye. *AB* 39 (1921): 241-276. PL 8.686-88. Maier, pp. 46-57. Musurillo, pp. 266-71.

The Acts of the Abitinian Martyrs: Acta Martyrum Saturnini, Felicis, Dativi, Ampelii et aliorum. In PL 8.689B-703B and PL 8.703C-715B. Maier, pp. 57-92. *Passio ss. Dativi Presb. et Aliorum.* Edited by Pio Franchi de'Cavalieri. *Studi e Testi* 65 (1935): 47-71. Manuscripts: Bibliothèque Nationale Latin Manuscripts 5297, 5318, 9714, 17625; Trier 1152; Montepessulanus (Montpellier) 1.

The Donatist Passion of Cyprian: S. Thasci Cypriani Opera Omnia. Opera Spuria. Edited by Guilelmus [William] Hartel. CSEL 3/3. Vienna: Geroldi, 1871. Maier, pp. 122-26. Reitzenstein, "Die Nachrichten," pp. 12-17.

The Martyrdom of Marculus: Passio Benedicti Martyris Marculi. PL 8.760-66. Maier, pp. 275-91.

The Passion of Maximian and Isaac: Passio Ss. Martyrum Maximiani et Isaac. PL 8.767-74. Maier, pp. 256-75.

The Passion of Saints Maxima, Donatilla and Secunda: Passio SS. Maximae, Donatillae et Secundae in *Passiones Tres Martyrum Africanorum.* Edited by Charles de Smedt. *AB* 9 (1890): 107-134. Maier, pp. 92-105.

A Sermon Given on the Passion of Saints Donatus and Advocatus: PL 8.752-58. Maier, pp. 198-211.

B: General Collections

Maier, Jean-Louis. Editor and translator. *Le Dossier du Donatisme.* T&U 134 and 135. Berlin: Akademie-Verlag, 1987 and 1989.

Herbert Musurillo. Editor and translator. *The Acts of the Christian Martyrs*. Oxford: Clarendon, 1972.

Migne, Jacques Paul. Editor. *Patrologiae Cursus Completus, Series Latina*. 221 vols. Paris: Garnier, 1844-94.

II. Related Texts and translations

Actes de la Conférence de Carthage en 411. Edited by Serge Lancel. SC 194, 195, 224, and 383. Paris: Cerf, 1972-1991; and CCSL 149A.

The Acts of St. Cyprian. In Musurillo, pp. 168-75.

The Ante-Nicene Fathers. Translations of the Writings of the Fathers down to A.D. 325. Edited by Alexander Roberts and James Donaldson. Buffalo: Christian Literature Publishing Co., 1885-1906; repr. Peabody, MA: Hendrickson, 1994.

Augustine. *Breviculus Collationis cum Donatistis*. In *Gesta Conlationis Carthaginensis, anno 411. Accedit Sancti Augustini breviculus conlationis cum Donatistis*. Edited by Serge Lancel. CCSL 149A. Turnhout: Brepols, 1974.

_____. *St. Augustin* [sic]: *The Writings against the Manichœans and against the Donatists*. Translated by J. R. King, revised and annotated by Chester D. Hartraft. Vol. 4 of *A Select Library of the Nicene and Post-Nicene Fathers*. First Series. Edited by Philip Schaff. Buffalo: Christian Literature Publishing Co., 1887; repr. Peabody, MA: Hendrickson, 1994.

_____. *Sancti Aurelii Augustini In Iohannis Euangelium Tractatus CXXIV*. Edited by D. Radbodus Willems. CCSL 36. Turnhout: Brepols, 1954.

_____. *Sancti Aurelii Augustini Ennarationes in Psalmos I-L*. Edited by Eligius Dekkers and Johannes Fraipont. CCSL 38. Turnhout: Brepols, 1956.

_____. *Sancti Aureli Augustini Scripta contra Donatistas*. Edited by M. Petschenig. CSEL 51-53. Vienna: Tempsky; and Leipzig: Freytag, 1908-10.

Concilia Africae A. 345 - A. 525. Edited by C. Munier. CCSL 149. Turnhout: Brepols, 1974.

Corpus Inscriptionum Latinarum. Volume VIII: *Inscriptiones Africae Latinae*. Edited by Gustavus Willmans. Berlin: Georg Reimerum, 1881.

Cyprian. *S. Thasci Cypriani Opera Omnia*. Edited by Guilelmus [William] Hartel. CSEL 3/1-3. Vienna: Geroldi, 1871. ANF 5.

_____. *St. Cyprian. The Lapsed. The Unity of the Catholic Church*. With translation and commentary by Maurice Bèvenot. Ancient Christian Writers 25. Westminster, Maryland: Newman; and London: Longmans, Green, 1957.

Eusebius. *The Ecclesiastical History*. 2 vols. Translated by J. E. L. Oulton. Loeb Classical Library. Cambridge: Harvard; and London: Heinemann, 1980.

_____. *Life of Constantine*. In *A Select Library of the Christian Church: Nicene and Post-Nicene Fathers*. Second series. Edited by Philip Schaff and Henry Wace. Vol. 1: *Eusebius: Church History, Life of Constantine the Great, and Oration in Praise of Constantine*. Translated by Arthur Cushman McGiffert. Buffalo: Christian Literature Company, 1890; repr. Peabody, MA: Hendrickson, 1994.

Gesta apud Zenophilum. In Optatus.

Hennecke, Edger. *New Testament Apocrypha*. Edited by Wilhelm Schneemelcher. English translation by R. McL. Wilson. 2 vols. Philadelphia: Westminster, 1962.

The Institutes of Gaius. Edited and translated with a commentary by Francis De Zulueta. 2 vols. Oxford: Clarendon, 1946 and 1953.

Justin. *Dialogue of Justin, Philosopher and Martyr with Trypho, A Jew*. In *ANF*. Vol. 1: *The Apostolic Fathers, Justin Martyr, Irenaeus*. Translated by A. Cleveland Coxe.

Lactantius. *On the Manner in Which the Persecutors Died*. In *ANF* Vol. 7: *Lactantius, Venantius, Asterius, Victorinus, Dionysius, Apostolic Teaching and Constitutions, 2 Clement, Early Liturgies*. Translated by A. Cleveland Coxe.

_____. *De morte persecutorum*. In *L. Firmiani Lactanti Opera Omnia*. Edited by S. Brandt and G. Laubman. CSEL 27. Prague and Vienna: Tempsky; and Leipzig, Freytag, 1893.

Liber Genealogicus. In *Monumenta Germaniae Historica Auctores Antiquissimi. Vol. 9: Chronica Minora Saec. IV. V. VI. VII*. Edited by Theodore Mommsen. Berlin: Weidmann, 1892; reprint ed., Munich: Strauss and Cramer, 1981.

Macrobius. *De singularitate clericorum*. In Cyprian. *S. Thasci Caecili Cypriani Opera Omnia*. CSEL 3/3.

Optatus of Milevis. *S. Optati Milevitani Libri VII*. Edited by Carolus Ziwza. CSEL 26. Prague and Vienna: Tempsky; and Leipzig: Freytag, 1893.

_____. *The Work of St. Optatus Bishop of Milevis against the Donatists*. Translated by O. R. Vassall-Phillips. London and New York: Longmans Green, 1917.

Pontius. *The Life and Passion of Cyprian*. In *ANF* Vol. 5: *Fathers of the Third Century: Hippolytus, Cyprian, Caius, Novatian, Appendix*. Translated by A. Cleveland Coxe.

_____. *Vita Caecili Cypriani*. In Cyprian. *S. Thasci Caecili Cypriani. Opera Omnia*. CSEL 3/3.

Tertullian. *Quintii Septimi Florentis Tertulliani Opera Omnia*. Edited by E. Dekkers. CCSL 1 and 2. Turnhout: Brepols, 1953. ANF 3-4.

The Theodosian Code. Translated with a commentary by Clyde Pharr. Princeton: Princeton University, 1952.

Tyconius. *The Book of Rules of Tyconius*. Edited by F. C. Burkitt. Cambridge: University Press, 1894.

_____. *Tyconius: The Book of Rules*. Edited with a translation by Willian S. Babcock. Texts and Translations 31. Early Christian Literature Series 7. Atlanta: Scholars, 1989.

Vita Caecilii Cypriani. In Cyprian. *S. Thasci Cypriani. Opera Omnia*. CSEL 3/3.

III. Commentaries and Notes on the Texts in this Volume

Dolbeau, François. "La Passion des saints Lucius et Montanus: Histoire et édition du texte." *REA* 29 (1983): 39-65. Includes notes on "A Sermon on the Passion of Saints Donatus and Advocatus."

Duncan-Jones, R. "An African Saint and his Interrogator." *Journal of Theological Studies* 25/2 (1974): 106-110.

Duval, Noël. "Une nouvelle édition du 'Dossier du Donatisme' avec traduction française." *REA* 35 (1989): 171-79.

Franchi de'Cavalieri, Pio. "Della 'Passio sanctarum Maximae, Donatillae et Secundae.'" *Note Agiografiche VIII.* In *Studi e Testi* 65 (1935): 76-97.

_____. *Passio ss. Dativi Presb. et Aliorum. Studi e Testi* 65 (1935): 1-46.

Reitzenstein, Richard. "Bemerkungen zur Märtyrliteratur. II). Nachträge zu den Akten Cyprians." *Nachrichten de königlischen Gesellschaft der Wissenschaften zu Göttingen*, Phil.-hist. Klasse 1919: 12-219.

_____. "Ein donatistisches Corpus cyprianischer Schriften." *Nachrichten de königlischen Gesellschaft der Wissenschaften zu Göttingen*, Phil.-hist. Klasse 1914: 85-92

Schäferdiek, Knut. "Der *Sermo de passione sanctorum Donati et Advocati* als donatistisches Selbstzeugnis." In *Oecumenica et Patristica: Festschrift für Wilhelm Schneemelcher zum 75. Geburstag.* Edited by Damaskinos Papandreou, Wolfgang A. Bienert and Knut Schäferdiek. Stuttgart, Berlin and Cologne: W. Kohlhammer, 1989.

IV. Secondary Studies

Aigrain, Rene. *L'Hagiographie: Ses sources, ses methods, son histoire.* Paris: Bloud & Gay, 1953.

Alexander, J. S. "Aspects of Donatist Scriptural Interpretation at the Conference of Carthage." T&U 128. *Studia Patristica* 15 (1984): 125-30.

Barnes, Timothy D. *Constantine and Eusebius.* Cambridge and London: Harvard, 1981.

Bauer, Walter. *Rechtgläubigkeit und Ketzerei im ältesten Christentum.* Tubingen: Mohr Siebeck, 1934. In translation as *Orthodoxy and Heresy in Earliest Christianity.* Edited by Robert A. Kraft and Gerhard Krodel. Philadelphia: Fortress, 1971.

Brisson, Jean-Paul. *Autonomisme et Christianisme dans l'Afrique romaine de Septime Sévère à l'invasion vandale.* Paris: Boccard, 1958.

_____. *Glorie et misére de l'Afrique chrétienne.* Paris: Laffont, 1948.

Brown, Peter. *Augustine. A Biography.* Berkeley and Los Angeles: University of California, 1967.

_____. "Religious Coercion in the Later Roman Empire: The Case of North Africa." *History* 48 (1963): 83-101 = *Religion and Society in the Age of Augustine*. London: Faber and Faber, 1972: 237-59.

Cagnat, René. *L'Armée romaine d'Afrique et l'occupation militaire de l'Afrique sous les empereurs*. Paris: Imprimerie nationale, 1913; repr. New York: Arno, 1975.

Carnazza-Rametta, Giuseppe. *Studio sul diritto penale dei Romani*. Messina, 1893; repr. Rome: "L'Erma" di Bretschneider, 1972.

Clark, Gillian. *Women in Late Antiquity: Pagan and Christian Lifestyles*. Oxford: Clarendon, 1993.

Crook, J. A. *Law and Life in Rome*. Ithaca: Cornell, 1967.

Delehaye, Hippolyte. "Contributions récentes à l'hagiographie de Rome et d'Afrique." *AB* 54 (1936): 298-300.

_____. "Review of Paul Monceaux, *L'épigraphie donatiste*." *AB* 29 (1910): 467-68.

De Veer, A. C. "L'exploitation du schisme maximianiste par Saint Augustin dans la lutte contre le Donatisme." *Recherches Augustiniennes* 3 (1965): 219-37.

Duval, Yvette. *Auprès des saints corps et âme: L'inhumation 'ad sanctos' dans la chrétienté d'Orient et d'Occident du IIIe au VIIe siècle*. Paris: Études Augustinennes, 1988.

Finkelstein, Louis. *Akiba: Scholar, Saint and Martyr*. New York: Covici, Friede, 1936; repr. Northvale, NJ, and London: Jason Aronson, 1990.

Frend, W.H.C. *The Donatist Church: A Movement of Protest in Roman North Africa*. Oxford: Clarendon, 1952.

_____. *Martyrdom and Persecution in the Early Church: A Study of Conflict from the Maccabees to Donatus*. New York: New York University, 1967. London: Faber and Faber, 1972.

_____. *The Rise of Christianity*. Philadelphia: Fortress, 1984.

_____. "The Seniores Laici and the Origins of the Church in North Africa." *Journal of Theological Studies* n.s. 12 (1961): 280-84.

_____, and Clancy, K. "When Did the Donatist Schism Begin?" *Journal of Theological Studies*, n.s., 28 (1977):104-9.

Hammond, N. G. L., and Scullard, H. H. Editors. *The Oxford Classical Dictionary*. 2nd ed. Oxford: Clarendon, 1970. S.v. " Dux," "Comites," and "Tribunus" by Henry M. D. Parker.

Kriegbaum, J. B. *Kirche der Traditoren oder Kirche der Märtyrer?* Innsbruck and Vienna: Tyrolia, 1986.

Lanata, Giuliana. *Gli atti dei martiri come documenti processuali.* Milan: Giuffrè, 1973.

————. *Processi contro Cristiani negle atti dei martiri.* 2nd ed. Turin: G. Giappichelli, 1989.

Lancel, Serge. "Les débuts du Donatisme: la date du 'Protocole de Cirta' et de l'élection épiscopale de Silvanus." *REA* 25 (1979): 217-29.

Markus, Robert A. *From Augustine to Gregory the Great: History and Christianity in Late Antiquity.* London: Variorum, 1983.

————. *Sacred and Secular: Studies on Augustine and Latin Christianity.* Aldershot, Hampshire: Variorum, 1994.

Martyns, Cées. "Les premiers martyrs et leurs rêves: cohesion de l'histoire and des rêves dans quelques 'passions' latins de l'Afrique du Nord." *Revue d'histoire ecclésiastique* 81/1-2 (1986): 5-46.

Meslin, Michel. "Vases sacrés et boissons d'éternité dans les visions des martyrs africains." In *Epektasis: Mélanges patristiques offerts au Cardinal Jean Daniélou.* Edited by Jacques Fontaine and Charles Kannengiesser. Paris: Beauchesne, 1972.

Monceaux, Paul. *Histoire littéraire de l'Afrique chrétienne depuis les origines jusqu'a l'invasion arabe.* 7 vols. Paris, 1901-23; repr. Brussels: Civilisation et Culture, 1963.

Pallu de Lessert, A. *Fastes des Provinces Africaines (Proconsulaire, Numidies, Maurétanies) sous la domination romaine.* Vol. 2: *Bas Empire.* Studia Historica 63. Paris: Leroux, 1901; repr. Rome: "L'Erma" di Bretschneider, 1969.

von Pauly, August Friedrich. *Paulys Realencyclopädie der classischen Alterumswissenschaft. Neue Arbeitung.* Edited by Georg Wissowa *et al.* Stuttgart: Metzler, 1893- . S.v. "Essig," by Hermann Stadler; and s.v. "Comites," "Dux," and "Tribunus," by Otto Seeck.

Pincherle, Alberto. "Un sermone donatista attribuito a s. Ottato di Milevi." *Bilychnis* 22 (1923): 134-48..

Raven, Susan. *Rome in Africa.* 3rd ed. London and New York: Routledge, 1993.

Romero Pose, E. "Medio Siglo de Estudios sobre el Donatismo (De Monceaux a nuestros dias)." *Salmaticensis* 19/1 (1982): 81-99.

Saxer, Victor. *Morts, martyrs, reliques en Afrique chrétienne aux pre-mieres siécles: Les temoignages de Tertullian, Cyprien et Augustin à la lumière de l'archéologie africaine.* Théologie historique 55. Paris: *Beauchesne*, 1980.

Ste Croix, G. E. M. de. "Why Were the Early Christians Persecuted?" In *Studies in Ancient Society.* Edited by M. I. Finley. In the *Past and Present Series.* Edited by Trevor Aston. London and Boston: Routledge and Kegan Paul, 1974.

Tengström, E. *Donatisten und Katholiken: Sociale, wirtschaftliche und politische Aspecte einer nordafrikanischen Kirchenspaltung.* Studia Graeca et Latina Gothoburgensia 18. Stockholm: Alqvist & Wiksell, 1952.

Tilley, Maureen A. "The Ascetic Body and the (Un)making of the World of the Martyr." *Journal of the American Academy of Religion* 59/3 (1991): 467-79.

_____. "Martyrs, Monks, Insects and Animals." In *The Medieval World of Nature: A Book of Essays.* Edited by Joyce E. Salisbury. New York and London: Garland, 1993: 93-107.

_____. "Scripture as an Element of Social Control: Two Martyr Stories of Christian North Africa." *Harvard Theological Review* 84/4 (1990): 383-397.

Trout, Dennis. "Re-textualizing Lucretia: Cultural Subversion in the *City of God.*" *Journal of Early Christian Studies* 2/1 (1994): 53-70.

INDEX

References to martyrs are given only if they occur
outside the story of their martyrdoms.

Duncan-Jones, R., 7-8

Dupin, Louis Elles, 62

Empedocles, 85 n.15

Euphrates, xxiii

Eusebius, church historian, xii, 7, 25

Felix, bishop and martyr, xiii ,xx, xxiii, xxviii

Florus, proconsul of Numidia, xxx

Fortuniatianus of Carthage, brother of the martyr Victoria, 42

Frend, W. H.C., xxx

Fundanus, bishop of Abitina, 30

Galerius, emperor, xxix, 13

Galerius Maximus, proconsul, 2-5

Gallienus, emperor, xxvii,13, 17, 18

Gaul, 51

Gratus, Catholic bishop of Car thage, xvi, xvii, xxv

Gregory the Great, xvii

Henchir Bou Cha, 7-8

Herrenianus, see Magnilianus

Honorius, emperor, xxxiii

Hosius of Cordoba, Catholic bish op, xvi, xxxi

Jerome, 13

Jesus, 13, 22

Justin, martyr, 79 n.7

Lactantius, xxviii,7

Lancel, Serge, viii, xiv n.7

Leontius, *dux* and later *comes,*

xxxii, 53

Licinius, emperor, 25

Mabillon, Jean, 62, 78

Macarius, imperial notary, xvi, xxv, xxxii, 78, 79

Maccabees, 44

Macrobius, Donatist bishop of Rome, 62, 75

Macrobius Candidatus of Carthage, 5

Magnilianus of Thibiuca, xxix, 8-10

Maier, Jean-Louis viii, 2, 8, 16, 17, 52, 62, 78

Majorinus, Donatist bishop of Carthage, xxv, 51

Marcellinus, tribune, 53

Marcellus of Theveste, martyr, xxviii

Marculus, xvii, xxi, xxiv

Marian and James, martyrs, 70 n.29

Mascula, xxx

Maxima, Donatilla and Secunda, xiii, xx, xxii, xxiii, xxiv, xxx, 25, 42, n52, 62

Maximian, emperor, xxvii, xxviii, 8, 13, 17, 18, 26

Maximian and Isaac, martyrs, xvii, xxi

Maximilian of Theveste, martyr, xviii, 59 n.13

Mensurius, Donatist bishop of Carthage, xi, xiv-xv, xxv, 25, 45, 46, 48

Migne, Jacques Paul, 62, 78

TRANSLATED TEXTS FOR HISTORIANS
Published Titles

Gregory of Tours: Life of the Fathers
Translated with an introduction by EDWARD JAMES
Volume 1: 176pp., 2nd edition 1991, ISBN 0 85323 327 6

The Emperor Julian: Panegyric and Polemic
Claudius Mamertinus, John Chrysostom, Ephrem the Syrian
edited by SAMUEL N. C. LIEU
Volume 2: 153pp., 2nd edition 1989, ISBN 0 85323 376 4

Pacatus: Panegyric to the Emperor Theodosius
Translated with an introduction by C. E. V. NIXON
Volume 3: 122pp., 1987, ISBN 0 85323 076 5

Gregory of Tours: Glory of the Martyrs
Translated with an introduction by RAYMOND VAN DAM
Volume 4: 150pp., 1988, ISBN 0 85323 236 9

Gregory of Tours: Glory of the Confessors
Translated with an introduction by RAYMOND VAN DAM
Volume 5: 127pp., 1988, ISBN 0 85323 226 1

The Book of Pontiffs (*Liber Pontificalis* to AD 715)
Translated with an introduction by RAYMOND DAVIS
Volume 6: 175pp., 1989, ISBN 0 85323 216 4

Chronicon Paschale 284–628 AD
Translated with notes and introduction by
MICHAEL WHITBY AND MARY WHITBY
Volume 7: 280pp., 1989, ISBN 0 85323 096 X

Iamblichus: On the Pythagorean Life
Translated with notes and introduction by GILLIAN CLARK
Volume 8: 144pp., 1989, ISBN 0 85323 326 8

Conquerors and Chroniclers of Early-Medieval Spain
Translated with notes and introduction by KENNETH BAXTER WOLF
Volume 9: 176pp., 1991, ISBN 0 85323 047 1

Victor of Vita: History of the Vandal Persecution
Translated with notes and introduction by JOHN MOORHEAD
Volume 10: 112pp., 1992, ISBN 0 85323 426 4

The Goths in the Fourth Century
by PETER HEATHER AND JOHN MATTHEWS
Volume 11: 224pp., 1992, ISBN 0 85323 426 4

Cassiodorus: *Variae*
Translated with notes and introduction by S. J. B. BARNISH
Volume 12: 260pp., 1992, ISBN 0 85323 436 1

The Lives of the Eighth-Century Popes (*Liber Pontificalis*)
Translated with an introduction and commentary by RAYMOND DAVIS
Volume 13: 288pp., 1992, ISBN 0 85323 018 8

Eutropius: Breviarium
Translated with an introduction and commentary by H. W. BIRD
Volume 14: 248pp., 1993, ISBN 0 85323 208 3

The Seventh Century in the West-Syrian Chronicles
Introduced, translated and annotated by ANDREW PALMER
including two Seventh-century Syriac apocalyptic texts
Introduced, translated and annotated by SEBASTIAN BROCK
with added annotation and an historical introduction by ROBERT HOYLAND
Volume 15: 368pp., 1993, ISBN 0 85323 238 5

Vegetius: Epitome of Military Science
Translated with notes and introduction by N. P. MILNER
Volume 16: 208pp., 2nd edition 1996, ISBN 0 85323 910 X

Aurelius Victor: De Caesaribus
Translated with an introduction and commentary by H. W. BIRD
Volume 17: 264pp., 1994, ISBN 0-85323-218-0

Bede: On the Tabernacle
Translated with notes and introduction by ARTHUR G. HOLDER
Volume 19: 176pp., 1994, ISBN 0-85323-368-3

The Lives of the Ninth-Century Popes (*Liber Pontificalis*)
Translated with an introduction and commentary by RAYMOND DAVIS
Volume 20: 360pp., 1995, ISBN 0-85323-479-5

Bede: On the Temple
Translated with notes by SEÁN CONNOLLY,
introduction by JENNIFER O'REILLY
Volume 21: 192pp., 1995, ISBN 0-85323-049-8

Pseudo-Dionysius of Tel-Mahre: *Chronicle*, Part III
Translated with notes and introduction by WITOLD WITAKOWSKI
Volume 22: 192pp., 1995, ISBN 0-85323-760-3

Venantius Fortunatus: Personal and Political Poems
Translated with notes and introduction by JUDITH GEORGE
Volume 23: 192pp., 1995, ISBN 0-85323-179-6

Donatist Martyr Stories: The Church in Conflict in Roman North Africa
Translated with notes and introduction by MAUREEN A. TILLEY
Volume 24: 144pp., 1996, ISBN 0 85323 931 2

For full details of Translated Texts for Historians, including prices and ordering information, please write to the following:
All countries, except the USA and Canada: Liverpool University Press, Senate House, Abercromby Square, Liverpool, L69 3BX, UK (*Tel* 0151-794 2233, *Fax* 0151-794 2235).
USA and Canada: University of Pennsylvania Press, Blockley Hall, 418 Service Drive, Philadelphia, PA 19104-6097, USA (*Tel* (215) 898-6264, *Fax* (215) 898-0404).